Economics of Fulfillment

Economics of Fulfillment

The Obsolescence of Socialism and Capitalism
and an Economic Philosophy for the Future

Threshold to Meaning Series
Book Two

VINCENT FRANK BEDOGNE

WIPF & STOCK · Eugene, Oregon

ECONOMICS OF FULFILLMENT
The Obsolescence of Socialism and Capitalism
and an Economic Philosophy for the Future

Threshold to Meaning, Book 2

Wipf & Stock
A Division of Wipf and Stock Publishers
199 W. 8th Ave., Suite 3
Eugene, OR 97401
www.wipfandstock.com

ISBN 13: 978-1-55635-925-5

Manufactured in the U.S.A.

In socialism, the individual has no motivation to contribute to the economy other than social and political conformity.

In capitalism, the individual is motivated by the artificial construct of money and profit.

In Economics of Fulfillment, the individual is motivated by his or her passion.

Contents

Illustrations

Preface

A S DIVERSE AS OUR individual experiences of life may be, we share the quest to negotiate life's course. We each, in our own way, venture from day to day, from event to event, from pivotal moment to pivotal moment, experiencing the pain and satisfaction of existence as we do. In the first book in this series, *Threshold to Meaning: Book 1, Evolution of Consciousness*, we delved into the nature of this journey. We described the universe as an evolution of consciousness that manifested in an evolution of matter and that advanced through the cycles, thresholds, trial and error, and creative building on and discarding of the old that characterizes a fundamental creative process. We detailed the stages of the universe's evolution and then went on to define the human role in that evolution. In the present book, we go beyond the broad and deeply philosophical views put forth in the first volume and delve into a pragmatic aspect of existence brought into focus by these views, one that in a direct manner is poised to transform the way we go about our lives. The topic is economics.

The mention of "economics" brings to mind many thoughts. We reflect on our struggle to feed, cloth, shelter, and educate our families and ourselves. We ponder our desire for material possession and our drive to advance to a higher social and economic status. Visions of budgets, politics, economic policy, and economic and military conflict between nations and classes flood our mind. Is this economics or is there something more?

Today, two major economic philosophies form the basis of our global economy—both embraced to some degree by every nation and by every government. They are *socialism* and *capitalism*—of which, in most nations, the latter, capitalism, has emerged as the dominate ideology. Does either system of economic belief, however, meet our needs? Does the economic activity of the state address the concerns of the state's citizenry? Does the economic activity of the multinational corporation meet the demands of nations?

On this point, there can be no argument. Few of us are content with our economic well-being. We cannot deny the vast inequalities of wealth and opportunity that exist between individuals and between nations. We cannot turn away from the political and military ramifications created by these divisions. There is hunger in the world. There is injustice in the world. There is oppression in the world. But, we ask, what alternative do we have? Faced with problems under capitalism, we look for solutions in socialism and central control. Faced with problems under socialism, we look for solutions in capitalism and free markets. The economic system to which our sentiments lean may not be perfect—we tell ourselves in justification of whatever ideology we may embrace—but it is the best we know.

In this book, we begin with a simple idea. It is the belief that we can do better. It is the notion that we can create an economic philosophy more vital than any in the past or of any in existence today—an economic doctrine better able to meet our material and spiritual needs than socialism or capitalism. The book is based on the premise that humankind has the means and the ability to create an economic ideology that fulfills the physical needs of every human being and that satisfies the even more deeply rooted needs we share as evolving beings in an evolving universe. I call this system of economic belief *Economics of Fulfillment*.

As such, the book is not an economics work in the traditional sense. As the second book in the *Threshold to Meaning* series, it expands on a key outcome of the evolution of consciousness account of the universe developed in the first book and, for this reason, is intimately connected to that book. It is possible to read *Economics of Fulfillment* without the background of the prior work—and, knowing that many will, I have done my best to make it accessible as such—but the topic's depth and greater meaning will be lost. In this regard, the reader will find periodic references to the first book, a less than ideal but necessary tactic to support ideas that to fully develop and justify would be beyond the scope of the present work. Moreover, the reader of traditional economic texts will find the treatise more esoteric than he or she may be accustomed. There are no graphs plotting supply, demand, inflation, interest rates, money supply, or other variable of traditional economic concern. Conversely, the reader of the first book will find *Economics of Fulfillment* more matter-of-fact than he or she may have anticipated. This reader, though, may rest assured. Much of the text is devoted to the nuts and bolts of economic function, but economic function rests on an underlying philosophy. Economics of fulfillment is not an economic ideology as we think of one today. It is an economic ideology as we will think of one tomorrow—an economic system of beliefs for the people that, as we cross the universe's threshold to meaning, we today are becoming.

In Part One, *Scarcity-Based Economics,* and in chapter one, *Freedom,* which establishes the first part of the book, we provide the background necessary to develop the ideas that follow. We highlight the evolution of consciousness view, explore the origin and meaning of resource scarcity, trace the evolution of economic thought and practice from the first urban community through the city, state, and nation-state, and examine our current level of social and economic organization—our blend of socialistic and capitalistic economic practices.

In Part Two, *Economics of Fulfillment,* we outline the economic philosophy our understanding of history and evolution—and the insight into the human condition it provides—leads us to conclude is poised to unfold. We identify the assumptions on which our vision of economics is based and the principle to which it must adhere. We outline a system of economic practice designed to function under the economics of fulfillment blanket and explore the values and beliefs we must embrace for our vision to unfold—the real-world feasibility of our economic ideals.

In Part Three, *Implementation,* we put theory and wisdom into practice, or at least we look at how we might do so. In what way will the first economics of fulfillment systems begin and how will these systems interact with existing socialist and capitalist economies? What educational and governmental structures must we put into place to allow the individual to thrive in an economics of fulfillment world? And how must we design these structures to allow economics of fulfillment systems to expand and to evolve from traditional economic systems?

In Part Four, *Freedom,* we look beyond the initial stages of implementation and explore the rebirth of global economics. We speculate on the decline and collapse of socialism and capitalism, the end of money, taxation, class structure, and the economic limits that we today take as immutable. We look at what human society will evolve to become and lay out a plan for social and economic reorganization without the conflict and upheaval that throughout history has defined the rebuilding of nations and cultures.

As we study evolution and the history of economics, as we reinvent economic theory, and speculate on where our ideas will take us, we are struck by a realization. Never again will we see economics in the light of despair. The economy of the future will not be dominated by politics, conflict, and regulatory control. It will not function through ideals of scarcity, competition, and a struggle to survive. There will be no winners and losers, divisions of opportunity, class and economically driven military turmoil. The economy of the future will not be based on socialistic ideals of collectivity and subservience to the state. The economy of the future will not be defined by capitalistic booms that soar to ever-greater reaches only to collapse into ever more inequitably felt recessions. The economy of the future will not be an intangible system where no economic model can predict its behavior, where no government policy can steer its course, and where the greed or psychological whim of a few can unleash economic devastation on the masses. The economy of the future is ours to create. It is an ideology of our invention, molded by the purity of our desire to fulfill our evolving personal and human needs.

1

Freedom

WE BEGIN THE TASK of economic reinvention with a simple but essential observation. We cannot separate our understanding of economic practice from our understanding of a basic human need. The need of which we speak is not physical. Our experience of it is affected by our economic situation, but the need itself exists on a deeper level than our drive for food, clothing, and shelter. At times, we may deny our experience of this need; but, in the absence of its fulfillment, we can never fully put it out of mind. It is a need that has fueled social transformation throughout the ages, a yearning we all share—the human drive for freedom.

To understand our need for freedom and the insight into economics it provides we must establish the context. We must devote a few paragraphs to the ideas developed in the first book in this series, *Threshold to Meaning: Book 1, Evolution of Consciousness*. This may appear to be a philosophical tangent—and the reader who expects the book to begin with an introduction to supply, demand, interest rates, federal reserve policy, consumer price index, or other traditional aspect of economic practice will find it deeply philosophical—but in the end it will prove fundamental. Unlike socialism and capitalism, economics of fulfillment is not merely a scheme to balance wants with resources. It is an aspect of a deeper transformation that is taking place within humanity.

Those who strive to understand the universe, which is all of us to a degree, have traditionally probed the workings of nature on two levels: the external and the internal. The external is the physical or objective side of existence. It is matter, energy, cause and effect, what we see, measure, and deal with in a tangible way. The internal is the nonphysical or subjective side of existence. It is emotion, creativity, consciousness, and our experience of or our belief in a god, soul, and afterlife. To explore the universe's internal side, we find ourselves drawn to theology and to its many philosophical divisions and offshoots, popular and traditional. Science, on the other hand, has evolved as the tool we use to explore the universe's external side.

As a result of this dichotomy in perspective and of the dominant position science occupies in our lives, most of us have grown up to think of the universe in external terms. The prevailing view at present is that the universe is the product of physical interaction—accounted for by the big bang model of cosmic formation and by the natural selection model of organic evolution. The universe's fundamental nature, as we have been taught, is as an evolution of matter that, with the advent of life, achieved the complexity to manifest in consciousness.

During the first half of the twentieth century, the French scientist and philosopher *Pierre Teilhard de Chardin* challenged this point of view.[1] A Jesuit priest trained as a paleontologist, Teilhard felt that no explanation of the universe would be complete, and therefore true to reality, that did not address the universe's external and internal dimensions. At times, we may find it useful to separate one point of view from the other, but any overall explanation of the universe must embrace its objective and subjective qualities. In no other way, Teilhard felt, can we understand the universe and the role humankind and we as individuals occupy in the universe.

Driven by this conviction, and despite the disapproval of the Church, Teilhard accepted the fossil evidence of organic evolution and participated in some of the twentieth century's most celebrated archeological expeditions. Teilhard firmly embraced the idea of organic evolution but reasoned that it did not take place through the purely external process of natural selection, as science had professed since the 1859 publication of Charles Darwin's *On the Origin of Species*, but in a different way—through the creative process, through the same creative mechanism that functions in the human being. Humanity is a part of the universe. We are an outcome of evolution. The creative process we experience, Teilhard believed, must in some respect be the same as the creative process that brought us into existence. On one level, the same process must be at work when the universe creates a star, galaxy, species, or ecosystem as is at work when a human being writes a novel, drafts a blueprint, composes a symphony, or invents a scientific theory.

1. See *Book 1, Evolution of Consciousness*, Preface and Series Introduction.

This realization led Teilhard to an even more startling conclusion. He reasoned that if the universe evolved through the creative process, through the same mechanism that functions in the human being, the universe's nature could not be as an evolution of matter. The universe must exist on another plane. A state of being more fundamental than matter must lie beyond what we observe and measure. Teilhard did not see the universe as an evolution of matter that with the advent of life achieved the complexity to manifest in consciousness. He saw the universe in a way that embraced its external and internal dimensions, as an evolution of consciousness that in the beginning and at every level of its becoming manifested in an evolution of matter.

Teilhard presented his *evolution of consciousness* vision of the universe in his book *The Phenomenon of Man*. Following Teilhard's death in 1955 and the book's publication shortly after, his ideas drew a great deal of popular and academic interest. The evolution of consciousness view tied together our fragmented understanding of the universe in an overall vision of evolution. But, as the years past, Teilhard's ideas fell into obscurity. Organized religion dismissed Teilhard's thought because it challenged scriptural notions of creation. Science dismissed Teilhard's thought because it challenged Darwinism and suggested that the universe's fundamental nature could not be quantified and boiled down to the simple relationships expressed in a mathematical equation.

The Jesuit's vision may have been intriguing and may have rang-true on an intuitive level, but it fell short in one significant way. Teilhard could not explain how the creative process functioned, how his "evolution of consciousness" took place. He offered no explanation as to how a universe whose nature is as an evolution of consciousness could manifest in the evolution of matter we see around us and science is devoted to understanding.

In the first book in this series, I picked up where Teilhard left off. I began with his vision of the universe and then went on to propose a simple mechanism, the *creative process*, that in a pragmatic and logic-driven way explains how our universe, taken to be as an evolution of consciousness, manifested in the evolution of matter we see around us and that clearly took place in the past. As a refresher, *Figure 1*, taken from that book, summaries the cyclic aspect of the creative process.

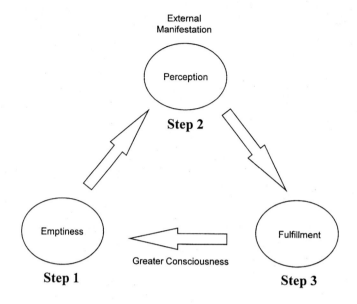

Fig. 1. The Creative Cycle. On its most basic level, the creative process consists of cycles and thresholds. The diagram illustrates the three steps of the creative cycle.

I then offered an account of the universe's origin, evolution, and immediate and ultimate future as I felt it would appear in light of the proposed unifying process. When we look at the universe in this way, it appears different from the way we are accustomed to seeing it. We no longer theorize evolution as taking place gradually, or linearly, accounted for by random forces and external interaction, Darwinian or otherwise. We theorize evolution as taking place through a process of groping, trial and error, creative cycles and thresholds, and a growth and collapse of uncertainty that gives rise to a building on and creative discarding of the old to create the new.

In this view, evolution progresses in two directions. As *Figure 2*, also taken from the first book, highlights, evolution's forward arrow thrusts ahead in time. It drives the universe to states of greater organization and consciousness. As it does, evolution's trailing arrow adapts the past. It reshapes and discards prior evolutionary forms in support of evolution's leading edge.

To lesser complexity and consciousness

To greater complexity and Consciousness

Fig. 2. Evolution's Two Arrows. Locked forever in the present, the leading arrow of the universe's overall creative process advances evolution toward greater complexity and consciousness while the trailing arrow advances evolution toward less complexity and consciousness.

In this process of building on and creatively discarding the old to create the new, the majority of evolutionary thresholds were small, barely discernible transformations that delineated the flow of time. Others were large—sweeping developments built on smaller ones that thrust the universe to altogether new levels of evolutionary development. Such thresholds allow us to divide evolution into five major periods or evolutionary stages: the universe's ages of *Emergence, Structure, Life, Understanding,* and *Fulfillment.*

With regard to the most recent of these periods, the universe, in the neighborhood of one hundred thousand years ago,[2] crossed the threshold to *Reflection*—the moment when the universe, through the evolution of the human psyche, became conscious of its existence and by doing so transcended the age of life and entered its current evolutionary era, the age of understanding. We embraced a distance within our being. We became aware we were aware, conscious we were conscious, beings curious as to the nature and purpose of our existence. Today the universe faces another, no less significant, turning point in the course of its development, the breakthrough moment that as I write these words thrusts evolution beyond the

2. See *Book 1, Evolution of Consciousness,* chapter 10.

age of understanding and into its final evolutionary period, the era I called fulfillment. Today, the universe crosses the *Threshold to Meaning*.

Like the transcendence to reflection, the crossing of this threshold unfolds within the human being. It represents our transformation to a higher state of existence, our leap to a more evolved level of awareness. Endowed with meaning, we are not only aware of our consciousness we are aware of our evolution. In a manner no less intrinsic than our sense of self, we internalize the course that brought us into existence. In a way no less second nature than our sentience, we embrace the universe's origin, transformation, and immediate and ultimate future. We embody the purpose of our existence, the reason for our being. We embrace meaning.

We also gain a perspective on economics that allows us to in a concise, though philosophical manner, contrast the economic practices of the past and of the present with the economic practices of the future. Socialism, capitalism, and their variations are economic models that evolved during the latter centuries of the universe's age of understanding. They are the expression of an external, Darwinian, materialistic view of the world. Economics of fulfillment is not socialism or capitalism. It is not a reshuffling of past economic views and ideals. Economics of fulfillment is a dimension of the evolutionary transformation taking place within us, a manifestation of the way people will see themselves and their place in existence. It is an aspect of the threshold to meaning, an economics based on an internal, consciousness based, humanity as paramount view of the world—an economics for the age of fulfillment.

With this thought, we establish the background to return our discussion to the chapter's premise and delve into the one aspect of the human experience that more than any other defines this new approach to economics. Associated with the reshaping of consciousness taking place within us—with humanity's crossing of the threshold to meaning—is the intensification of a long-felt need, a desire we all share, a want that has driven history and that is essential to any understanding of or reinvention of economics—the human yearning for freedom.

To some freedom is a concept, a notion we associate with law and politics. To others freedom is a right or a privilege. We enjoy or at least strive to enjoy freedom of speech, freedom of government, freedom to live and work where we want. But freedom exists on a deeper plane. It has a meaning that embraces these and our other ideas about its character but that is not limited by these ideas or by the social context in which they exist. Freedom has an underlying significance, a fundamental nature that our evolution of consciousness view allows us to see.

As evolving beings in an evolving universe, we are compelled to grow and learn. It is our nature to reinvent ourselves, to aspire to higher states of existence. Evolution functions through the creative process. It takes place through the mechanism of cycles and thresholds, trial and error, and creative building on and discarding of the old that defines creative activity. For the universe to evolve—for us to learn and advance, for humankind to do what it must do and to become what it can become—we must have space. We must have room to reflect and express our thoughts and to put our thoughts into action. We must have the opportunity to reinvent our world and ourselves. This is the underlying nature of freedom. Freedom is the state of the universe where the creative process can function. Freedom is the environment that allows creativity to take place and humankind to advance. Freedom is central to the human experience. Without freedom, we languish. To deny freedom is to deny our humanity.

Yet, we face boundaries to our freedom. These boundaries may be political. The direction of our life may be dictated by law and government, imposed through the power of our police and military institutions. Boundaries to our creativity may be philosophical, dictated by religious and other beliefs that we impose on ourselves or that are imposed on us by tradition. Boundaries to our creativity may be social: norms of dress, speech, and behavior imposed by family and community. Boundaries to our creativity may also be within ourselves. At times, we all feel the need to cling to ideas and ways of doing things past their usefulness. We *stagnate*, or use our creative power to justify obsolete ideas for no other reason than they may once have been worthwhile.[3]

To some extent, boundaries are necessary. Though we may hold onto old ideas and old ways of doing things past their usefulness, respect for the traditional is worthwhile. Trial and error is a dimension of the creative process. We cannot function without it. We make mistakes, but if we did not learn from our mistakes—and, by doing so, limit the range of our trial and error—we would grope without end. We would forever reinvent the wheel. Boundaries structure the creative process. Without boundaries, evolution would flail, and we would wander in time.

---

3. See *Book 1, Evolution of Consciousness*, chapter 11.

Limits to our creative freedom are also necessary to prevent our actions from restricting the freedom and creative activity of others. To a degree, we all live subject to the power of the police state, and most of us see the police state and the myriad of laws it enforces as a restriction to our freedom. In many ways it is. But, at least in most parts of the world and at humanity's present point in evolution, the police state also helps ensure our safety and thus gives us a freedom to go about our lives in a way we would not otherwise enjoy. Less overt limits to our creative freedom also prevent our actions from restricting the creative freedom of others. Above all is the value we place on our individuality. Most of us enjoy the freedom to envision God and practice religion in our own way; but, out of respect for others, we limit the extent to which we impose our views on those around us.

Certain limits to our freedom are necessary; others are not. One limit in particular, we can no longer justify and must move beyond. Most of us face this limit, and it creates legal and political restrictions that limit the creative freedom we all enjoy. It is a boundary imposed on us by ideology, tradition, and by our fear of the future and our reluctance to look ahead. It is our adherence to the ideals of contemporary economic philosophy.

No matter what economic system we live under, whether it leans toward socialism or toward capitalism, our freedom—our ability to evolve and to advance the evolution of humanity—is restricted by economic concerns. We work to survive. We exist locked in a battle to provide for our families and for ourselves. We struggle against ever more pervasive corporate and government intrusion into and oversight of our activities. We live in a world that pits nations and individuals in a competition for resources that we have been indoctrinated to believe are scarce—a world where for every winner there must be a vast and growing number of losers. Rhetoric, wishful thinking, and the occasional success story aside, today's economic environment offers little chance for most of the global population to move beyond the circumstance of wealth imposed at birth. Socialism, capitalism, and the play between these ideologies have brought us to where we stand and over the centuries have elevated the human condition, but traditional economics has reached its functional end. For reasons that if not self-evident will become clear, today's economic ideals limit our evolution and the fulfillment it brings into our lives.

Freedom is essential to our ability to grow and create and to know the satisfaction that such brings. It is a prerequisite to our evolution. As such, freedom is central to our economic practices—as basic as food, clothing, and shelter. Economics of fulfillment is a manifestation of the way people will see themselves and their world in the years ahead, a measure of the extent to which we will demand and embrace freedom. Economics of fulfillment is a dimension of the evolutionary transformation taking place within us. It is an aspect of the universe's threshold to meaning—a system of economic ideals for the people we are today becoming. The human community evolves through the evolution of the individual. The universe evolves through the evolution of the human community. Freedom is the environment of the creative process, the state of surroundings that allows evolution to take place. It is the need that if not satisfied motivates humanity. Freedom is that to which this book is devoted to furthering. Freedom is the desire that when fulfilled—and that through the action of its fulfillment—opens the way into our future.

PART ONE

Scarcity-Based Economics

2

The Origin and Impact of Scarcity

A S THE PREVIOUS CHAPTER suggested, our understanding of economics is related to our view of the world and to the role we perceive ourselves as occupying in the world. In the first section of the book, we establish this connection. We describe the origin of economic activity, the evolution of economic thought, and the world's current economic practices and systems of economic belief. We present the background we need to carry our look at economics beyond ideas of supply and demand, haves and have-nots, and fiscal and monetary policy—beyond socialism and capitalism and the limited view of the world on which these systems are based.

With the dawn of the human ability to reflect, our ancient ancestors setout to explore and learn about their world. In doing so, they created a human experience rich in gods and spirits, rites and artistic expression. They formed families and family groups, nurtured sons and daughters, mourned the death of loved ones, and speculated on the passage into afterlife. Our ancient ancestors also pondered the workings of the physical world and faced the day-to-day concerns of existence. They required the economic basics—food, clothing, and shelter.

The earliest members of the human community met their physical needs by hunting and gathering. As hunters and gatherers, bands lived nomadically. They also occupied an ecological niche. As does say a baboon troop, bands maintained a place in an ecosystem. Our subsistence activities were integrated into the function of the biosphere. We enjoyed a place in nature, and nature gave us what we needed to fulfill our role in the ecosystem. Periods of hunger occurred when climates changed and ecosystems realigned. Bands died out or had to move on, but these developments were the exception. For the most part, the biosphere and our role in the ecosystem provided the material resources necessary for life. All we needed and desired was there for our taking.

As a result, the member of the early hunting and gathering band devoted relatively little time to subsistence activities. It is difficult to say how much, but anthropological studies of the hunting and gathering cultures that remained untouched by the outside world into the late nineteenth and early twentieth centuries suggest remarkably little. Time spent on subsistence activities varies with the ecosystem in which a band exists. A member of a band in a harsh ecosystem—such as the San, or African Bushman, who lived, and to some extent continue to subsist, in the Kalahari Desert of Botswana and Namibia where game is seasonal— spends somewhat more time hunting and gathering than a member of a band in a less rigorous environment—such as the Mbuti Pigmies who flourished in the Ituri rain forest of Central Africa or the Native American tribes of the United States Pacific Northwest who enjoyed an abundance of deer and salmon. On the whole, subsistence activities in the hunting and gathering band occupied a few hours a week, a fraction of the time spent by most members of modern economies.

Even more important, anthropological studies tell us that hunting and gathering people do not consider the time they spend providing for themselves work. In their eyes, life is not a struggle to survive. It is life. Work is only work when you would rather be doing something else and you know of something else to do. In the hunting and gathering band, subsistence activities are integrated into social, religious, and other activities. Nomadic bands engaged in trade. Many even used some form of money, or common item of exchange, but economics did not dominate life. Economics was important but was not the center of existence. It was not what life was about.

About twelve thousand years ago, the evolutionary advance took place that transformed this view of economics and its role in human existence. Groups moved away from a nomadic, ecologically integrated way of life and began to cluster in the first permanent settlements.[1]

To understand why we left our hunting and gathering ways, we need to draw on *Threshold to Meaning: Book 1, Evolution of Consciousness* and bring

---

1. The date of the first permanent settlements is generally taken to be about twelve thousand years ago. Though controversial, some anthropologists place this date as early as seventeen thousand years ago. Because the earliest settlements where primitive, there is also uncertainty as to what constitutes a permanent place of occupation as opposed to a village or other site lived in for part of the year to follow the migration of game or for a religious or other purpose.

in a central idea: *collectivization.*[2] A social bond is made when we perceive and are perceived as the object of the need to belong. Thus, the greater our sense of self—the greater our substance of character as individuals—the stronger the social bonds we can form. Over the course of evolution, human beings became more aware and individualistic. By this, we do not mean that we evolved to greater arrogance, narcissism, or self-absorption, though such aspects of our personality existed and matured. Rather, we evolved to greater individuality in the most fundamental sense: to greater personality, to greater autonomy and consciousness, to greater freedom of thought and willingness to explore, to greater recognition of ourselves and of our place with respect to one another and the human community. In response, our social relationships became more complex. Society advanced from more uniform, or collective, forms to more nestled, layered, and strongly bonded, or less collective, forms. *Figure 3* illustrates this trend in societal evolution.

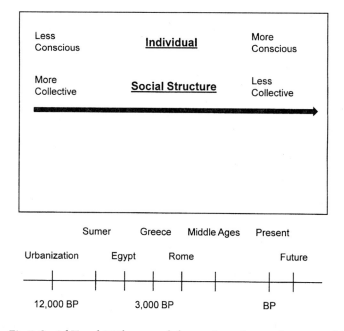

Fig. 3. Social Trend. With ups-and-downs along the way, human social structure has advanced from more uniform, or collective forms, that emphasized the communal, to more nestled and intimately bonded, or less collective forms, that emphasized the family and individual.

2. See *Book 1, Evolution of Consciousness,* chapters 5, 9, 10, and 11.

Families and bands joined to create larger, more complex groups, which joined to create communities. As communities grew, we reached the point where we could no longer sustain the intricacies of our social interaction while wandering the countryside and found it necessary to live in permanent settlements. Our move to urbanization was the result of a trend toward decollectivization traceable through human evolution, through life's evolution, and as far back as the universe's formative stages of structural evolution. We did not give up our nomadic way of life because we invented agriculture, which archeology tells us came sometime later, or for any other external cause. We gave it up because it was in our nature as the more conscious, highly evolved beings we had become to do so.

Where, then, did we build the first settlements and what might they have looked like? At one time, anthropologists believed urbanization began at a single spot called the "nuclear area" of the *fertile triangle*—the crescent that extends from the Nile Valley to the Tigris and Euphrates rivers—then diffused throughout the Near East, spread north into the Indus valley and China, westward into Europe, and across the Bering Strait into the Americas. Today, most scientists feel urbanization arose independently at these locations. In either view, the first settlements were little more than areas where people stayed for extended periods during their wanderings. These places may have been caves or clusters of shelters built near a stable source of food and water or near an area with religious significance. As time progressed, life revolved around these settlements. Driven be the need to form less collective communities, people felt the desire to be closer and chose to make the settlements their home.

This seemingly innocuous decision thrust economics to the forefront of the human experience. Only a limited amount of game could be hunted and fruits and tubers gathered within a reasonable distance from a settlement. As a result, we had to get food and other items in a different place from where we consumed them. With urbanization, human bands abandoned the ecological niche enjoyed when living nomadically. Our surroundings, our place in the works of the biosphere, no longer directly provided for our material needs. The community experienced a chronic shortage of food and other goods. It existed in a state of intrinsic *scarcity of recourses*.

Scarcity was a general condition in the early urban community. Inhabitants therefore found it necessary to devise systems to coordinate the way people gathered resources in the countryside, where they existed in surplus, and to divide them up in the village, where they existed in deficit. Scarcity was a fabrication created by urbanization and ecological isolation; but, from the vantage of those who lived in the community, it was the innate state of the world. The urban community brought into existence systems of economic activity based on the notion that resources are by nature limited and human material wants are by nature unlimited and that some mechanism must exist to encourage the production of goods and services and to regulate their allocation. Urbanization founded *scarcity-based* economics—economics as we typically think of it today.

At its essence, a scarcity-based economic system is a way to regulate human behavior. It is a set of rules and guidelines that—based on the supposition that resources are limited and human material wants are unlimited—assigns tasks and responsibilities and establishes how the material resources brought into existence by these tasks and responsibilities are divvied out. A scarcity-based economic system is an agreed upon way of conducting subsistence activities based on a mutually accepted view of the world.

How, then, did the population of the early urban community regulate the behavior of its members? To some extent, regulation took care of itself. Faced with hunger, the hunter is motivated to pick up his spear, and the toolmaker is motivated to chip a spear point. When someone needed something, they made, took, found, picked, killed, or traded for what they needed. To a degree, regulation took place on its own—through supply and demand, through what we today would call *market forces*.

Market forces alone, however, were not enough to regulate the economy of the early urban community. Under the dictates of the market, some members of the community—say those who were skilled hunters—would have plenty to eat while others—those with less hunting skill or those physically unable to hunt and with no skill to trade or with no friend or family member to provide for their needs—would go hungry. Left to the dictates of supply and demand, some members of the community would have more than they needed and others would not have enough. This disparity of wealth would create tension, and the social structure of the community would lose cohesiveness. To maintain the integrity of the community, and thus to further humankind's societal development and further the evolution of less collective social forms, everyone's needs had to be met, at least to the standards agreed on by the community. This required additional regulation. There had to be rules to direct individual behavior for the common good. For the community to be a community, some form of *central control* was also necessary.

Central control, of course, had its own consequences. We can imagine communities where everyone gathered by the village fire at night to figure out what needed to be done the next day and to assign the tasks to those best suited or to those who wanted to perform them. This situation certainly existed, but history and archaeology suggest that it was not generally the case. In a regulatory system, someone must make the rules. As communities grew larger and the need for resources grew more pressing, it became difficult for the community as a whole to perform this task. An element of the community was given, or more realistically took upon itself, the responsibility to figure out what was needed, who did what, and who received the benefits. Urbanization and the scarcity it created brought into being a *governing class*.

Those who made the rules, of course, had to have a way to make everyone else abide by them. To some extent, this took place through the social structure of the community. We accepted the rules made by our community leaders because we respected them and believed that they had our best interests at heart. But, as we see in the dynamics of any group, rarely does everyone feel their contribution is essential and appreciated. How many groups have we been in where every member felt that the people in charge were running things the right way? In the early urban community, those in power had to have a way to execute their power. In addition to a ruling class, scarcity-based economics required an *enforcing class*. Urbanization founded the rudiments of what we today would call the *police state*.

The emergence of a ruling and enforcing class, of course, brought with it the emergence of the class of individuals of which most were members. The ruling class governed. The enforcing class enforced. But, in the pure sense, neither group directly contributed to the material well-being of the community. They may have implemented and enforced the procedures that allowed economic activity to function more efficiently, but they did not perform that activity. They did not build the shelters and chip the spear points. They did not gut and skin the antelope. They only ate its meat. With the development of a ruling and enforcing class, there emerged another division in the economic fabric. Most in the community found themselves members of the *working class*.

In the hunting and gathering culture, social structure stood on its own. The individual occupied a place in society that only to a degree was associated with his or her economic contribution. With urbanization, society and economics melded. To a greater extent, our place in the community aligned with our economic status.

Along with economically based social structure, urbanization and scarcity brought into being a new view of the world. They inspired a vision of the universe and of the human being with ramifications so far reaching as to affect every generation that came after and that only today we have begun to evolve beyond.

For the first time in our existence, we did not see ourselves as part of our environment but in opposition to our environment. To us, existence was as a battle to eke out of the world what we needed to feed, cloth, and shelter ourselves. The Earth was our provider and our adversary, and we had to take from it what we needed and desired. The Europeans who settled North America, for example, saw the wilderness as a resource to be tamed and harnessed. In contrast, the largely nomadic native population saw the Earth as alive. The Earth was a being to be respected and worshipped, the nurturing spirit. Urbanization brought into existence the concept of *nature*, the idea that we are separate from the "natural" world. For us, life was a battle against the elements, a *struggle to survive*.

Urbanization and scarcity also changed our notion of work. No longer were subsistence activities inseparable from other aspects of our life. To a greater extent, we did not go about our activities because it was what we did, the purpose for our existence, that which we felt driven to do. We did not hunt and gather because it was our life. We hunted and gathered to sustain our life. Scarcity brought into being the concept of work and labor. With scarcity, subsistence increasingly became work and we increasingly became laborers.

As important, scarcity and urbanization changed our relationship to one another. Tension existed between ruling, enforcing, and working classes. The need to allocate food and other goods also placed individuals within a class at odds for the necessities of life. Conflict existed before urbanization, but as we will describe in Chapter Twelve, *Social Reformation*, tension in nomadic cultures largely revolved around territorial disputes between bands and social position in a band. It was a manifestation of our evolution to less collective forms of social structure—an outcome of the cycles and thresholds, the trial and error, and the buildup and collapse of uncertainty that defines the creative process. Scarcity melded into this algorithm of change the desire for material resources. It nurtured the idea of *competition*. It ingrained in us the notion that for every winner there must be one or more losers.

Our early ancestors required food, clothing, and shelter. The evolutionary drive to create less collective social structures brought urbanization. Urbanization and the separation between the human band and the ecosystem it spawned produced chronic scarcity. Scarcity spurred the development of systems to balance need with production and the social fabric and play between market forces and central control needed to sustain such systems. Scarcity and urbanization also brought into human consciousness a worldview dominated by ideals of man-against-nature and man against himself. Scarcity and urbanization ingrained in our being notions of class, wealth, property, survival, competition, and regulatory control. The economic practices founded in the first urban communities became the basis on which over the millennia we would create the global economy of today.

3

The Evolution of Economic Theory and Practice

A S COMPLEX AND IN many ways as little understood as today's global economy is, it rests on the worldview and social dynamics that resulted when we left our nomadic, hunting and gathering way of life and settled into a stationary, urban way of life. In one form or another, every nation embraces a scarcity-based economic philosophy. As any economic text will tell you, current economic ideology is predicated on the belief that resources are by nature limited and human material wants are by nature unlimited. Although the supposition of scarcity has to this point withstood time, the way in which we have accommodated it has changed.[1] Over the millennia and in particular over the last several centuries, we have invented a number of economic theories and philosophies and a number of economic models and systems to implement our theories and philosophies. A look at this economic evolution reveals something fundamental about the way we have conducted our economic affairs, an observation that stands out when one is aware of it but that is not often addressed in the economic literature. We see a trend in economic evolution—one that is important to recognize and that we will build on throughout the book.

To discern this inclination, we begin by tracing the development of economic practice. During the Egyptian, Greek, and Roman empires, systems with strict central control dominated economic life. A person in ancient Egypt saw his or her activities under the harsh management of a ruling class, the leaders of which often had the status of gods. Citizens also faced substantial taxes, restrictions, and obligations. In early Greece, Gelon of Syracuse, Periander of Corinth, Polycrates of Samos, and others

---

1. To a degree, mainstream economists have challenged the assumption of scarcity, and we will put it to the test in chapter 5, *Assumptions and Guiding Principle.*

in a line of so-called benevolent dictators oversaw economic activity. They maintained a high degree of control but to a greater extent than most rulers of their day used their power for the good of their people. In the Roman Empire, life was dominated by great estates called villas. On these estates, landlords supervised the cultivation of their land by slaves and former slaves. Workers and their heirs were required by imperial edict to remain on their lands and to serve their lords. As in Greek and Egyptian times, the power of the Roman Empire and its lords was maintained through a strong military class.

During the fifth century, the Roman Catholic Church and the aristocracy in the parts of Europe that would become England, Germany, and Scandinavia introduced a system of central control that dominated economic life in the West for almost a thousand years—*seignoralism*. In this system, a lord, or *seigneur*, headed an agricultural unit of production and consumption, or a farm that could meet the needs of its workers and overseers with limited trade and outside interaction. Through the power of an armed enforcing body, the seigneur judged, punished, and directed the actions of those under his jurisdiction, the *peasantry*, who worked the land.

By the thirteenth century, the rights of the peasants and the responsibilities of the seigneur were clearly defined. The peasants cultivated and harvested the lord's land, but were allowed to farm and even own some land to support themselves and their families. The peasants also had grazing rights and the rights to fuel and building materials, though not often the right to hunt. The lord had the right to tax his people, to take an inheritance tax at their deaths, and to reclaim their lands if they died without heirs. The seigneur also charged payment for the use of the lord's grain mill, bread oven, and other communal property. In some instances, seigneurs went so far as to charge payment for a peasant father to offer his daughters in marriage.

By the end of the middle ages, the rigid control of earlier periods had begun to break down. Peasants sold excess products to buy freedoms from lords, and lords replaced peasants, whom they had a lifelong commitment to care for, with cheaper wage laborers. By the late 1600s, seignoralism had largely disappeared, the deathblow dealt by the chill climate of the little ice age, waves of bubonic plague that periodically swept Europe, and the social upheaval and labor shortages these created. The seigneurs, though, remained socially dominant.

By the mid 1700s, the industrial revolution had taken hold. Rural communities broke apart, and people moved into cities and labored in factories. Subsistence no longer meant farming. It meant working for the wage needed to purchase the food and other items necessary to subsist. Though in one form or another money had been in use for millennia, to an extent never before experienced we embraced a monetary economy. Humanity had established the economic framework that would directly lead to the complex and interconnected economies of today.

To understand the significance of this event and to bring to its conclusion our goal to discern the trend in economic evolution that we spoke about earlier, we need to incorporate the development of economic theory and philosophy into our account of economic evolution.

Economic issues have occupied the human mind throughout the ages. In ancient Greece, Plato and Aristotle wrote about trade, wealth, property, and the difficulties of production and distribution. Modern economic theory takes us to the sixteenth century and to a form of economic activity called *mercantilism*. The objective of the mercantile economy was to increase the power and wealth of the nation, measured by a nation's stores of gold and silver. Since most European nations had little natural reserves of these metals, they had to be acquired through trade. This inspired policies to keep wages low and the population growing. A large, poorly paid population could produce more and cheaper trade goods and thus bring into the nation—or into the hands of its ruling elite—more gold and silver.

In the eighteenth century, *physiocracy* influenced economic thought. The physiocratic doctrine embraced free trade and the supremacy of natural law, order, and wealth. It also inspired the first serious attempt to study the nature of economic behavior. This was conducted by the British economist and philosopher *Adam Smith*; who, in his work *An Inquiry into the Nature and Causes of the Wealth of Nations*, founded the field of political economics and put forth many ideas that influence economic ideology to this day.

Smith's thought centered on freedom and the nature of capital. In particular, he felt that capital is best employed for the production and distribution of wealth without the interference of a monarch or other governing body. In Smith's view, the sources of all income are rent, wages, and profits. He felt that the production and exchange of goods could be stimulated and the general standard of living increased only by private industry with a minimum of government control and oversight. To justify this idea, Smith came up with one of the most debated statements in economic thought, the principle of the "invisible hand." In pursing his or her own good, Smith felt, every individual is led as if by an invisible hand to achieve the best good for all.

Smith's ideas of a free, or *laissez-faire*, economy founded the *classical school* of economic thought, furthered by David Ricardo, John Stuart Mill, and Thomas Robert Malthus. Classical economists believed in competition, free markets, private property, and minimum government regulation. If left alone, they felt, the economy would self-regulate to achieve the greatest benefit for everyone. Mill, however, in his *Principles of Political Economy*, accepted the need for some government oversight. Malthus, in his *An Essay on the Principle of Population*, felt that population would always exceed food production and must be limited by government policy. In most respects, however, the classical economists were not far apart in their views. They embraced the doctrine of the French economist Jean Baptiste Say known as "Say's Law of Markets." It holds that unemployment in a competitive economy will be negligible because supply creates demand up to the limit of human labor and natural resources.

Opposition to the classical school of economic thought came from early socialist writers including, in the 1800s, the philosopher Karl Marx. An exile from Germany, Marx spent most of his life in London, supported by his friend and collaborator Friedrich Engels. Marx, who was influenced by the German philosopher G. W. F. Hegal and by the deplorable working and living conditions that existed in Europe at the time, felt that the economy was not capable of regulating itself for the common good. In Marx's view, the economy consisted of two classes of people, the *capitalists*, who controlled the means of production, and the workers, or *proletarians*, who provided the labor. The goal of the capitalists was to use their capital—and the control over labor, material, and production resources it provided—to acquire the greatest amount of additional capital with the least amount of capital outlay.

In his *Communist Manifesto*, published in 1848, Marx concluded that the disparity of wealth between individuals and classes produced by capitalism would lead to its downfall. He saw capitalism as a transitional system that would be replaced by a communally based system called *socialism*. In socialism, a person's work was not rewarded based on competition and the market value of labor but according to an individual's need and contribution. Marx, however, felt that the capitalists would not give up their power and wealth without a fight and that socialism would only emerge following a revolution by the proletariat.

At about the same time as Marx, a development took place in the natural sciences that would have as profound of an influence on economic thought as any work in the field. England in the nineteenth century was an empire in the throes of the industrial revolution. As Marx had observed, life was hard and competitive. Men struggled to feed their families. Companies struggled to dominate their markets. International trade flourished, and nations struggled to extend their political and military influence around the globe. Into this atmosphere of social and economic conflict, the theory of evolution took root and the man most responsible for its development was born. In 1859, Charles Darwin published his *On the Origin of Species*.[2]

Darwin brought into human consciousness the notion of organic evolution, or change over time, and proposed a theory to account for that evolution, *natural selection*. In Darwin's natural selection model, mutations, or changes, are said to randomly occur in an organism and to create variations in organism structure. If these variations strengthen the organism, and it is better able to survive its environment and reproduce, it passes its improved characteristics to its offspring. Environment selects naturally occurring traits and thus drives organic evolution.

In light of the larger evolution of consciousness vision of the universe developed in *Threshold to Meaning: Book 1, Evolution of Consciousness*, what seems clear is that in his attempt to explain organic evolution—of which the event itself is supported by a vast body of fossil evidence—Darwin took the views of his culture—namely those of competition and a struggle to survive—and imposed those views on his observations of the natural world. Darwin filtered his observations through his worldview, its origins in the human move to urbanization and the condition of scarcity it created. Like human beings, organisms and species competed for resources. In nature, there were winners and losers, those who survive and prosper and those who do not.

This view had the catalytic effect of deepening our conviction in the ideals that gave rise to it. Darwin imposed a worldview brought into being by scarcity and urbanization on his observations of the natural world.

2. See *Book 1, Evolution of Consciousness*, chapters 9 and 12.

We then used Darwin's interpretations of the natural world to justify our worldview. In nature, we found a deep-seated rationalization for our economic struggle to survive—for our belief in the notion of competition, for our acceptance of the idea that there are those who come out on top and those who are left behind. Darwin solidified an external, materialistic vision of human existence. Social and economic interaction was survival of the fittest.

At about the same time as Marx and Darwin, there emerged the neoclassical school of economic thought. For the most part, neoclassical economists such as Leon Walrus, Karl Menger, and William Stanley Jevons, embraced the ideas of the classical school. They believed in low taxes, low public spending, and annually balanced budgets. Disparities in wealth, they felt, had nothing to do with class or the economic resources available to the individual. They were the result of differences in human beings—in talent, energy, ambition, and intelligence. They, however, felt that economic activity was influenced less by the supply of goods than the classical school felt and more by the demand for goods. In particular, they believed that the psychology of consumer choice, or our perceived as opposed to our actual needs, affected economic activity and introduced the concept of *utility*, or the satisfaction provided by marginal purchase.[3]

In the early 1900s, Marxist ideas took hold in Russia. And, after the stock market crash of 1929, the United States, Europe, and most other parts of the world plunged into the *Great Depression*. The duration and severity of this downturn perplexed economists and challenged the idea that a free-market economy would self-regulate to create full employment and to improve the general well-being. Classical economists argued that if left alone the depression would run its course and the economy would in time recover. But as the depression dragged on and political tensions increased, politicians leaned toward the view that classical economic theory could not account for economic behavior. Afraid that the depression would bring a spread of fascism and communism, leaders demanded a new economic model.

The British economist Alfred Maynard Keynes provided this model. In his work, *A Treatise on Money*, published in 1930, Keynes sought to

3. For the non-economist, the concept of utility can be understood with a simple example. If you were to buy one item, say a television, it would be quite valuable to you. If you were to buy two, in that you could only watch one at a time, the second would be less valuable. Marginally, it would provide less utility. The third, still less and so on.

explain why an economy operates unevenly, why it has periods of booms and recessions, or the ups-and-downs of what economists call the business cycle. In his most significant work, *The General Theory of Employment, Interest, and Money*, published in 1936, he put forth the idea that no self-correcting mechanism existed in the economy that could lift it out of a depression and that the only way to do this was through government intervention.

Because consumers were limited in the amount they could spend by their incomes, Keynes felt that they could not be the source of the booms-and-busts of the business cycle. Rather, the forces that influenced the business cycle were government spending and business investment. In a recession, government must encourage private investment and make up for any shortfall in private investment through government expenditure. In a mild economic contraction, a monetary policy of easy credit and low interest rates can stimulate investment and restore demand and employment. More severe contractions require deficit spending by government with the money used to fund public works projects and to subsidize the groups most affected.

United States President Franklyn Delano Roosevelt adopted Keynesian policy and initiated a variety of federally-funded jobs and other programs to put it into practice. These ranged from projects to improve the health of forest and agricultural land to major infrastructure projects such as the construction of dams, highways, and irrigation systems. Although these, *New Deal*, programs were of unquestionable benefit to the individuals they employed, and the nation is still reaping benefits from the Hoover Dam and other large public works projects, it was not until the fundamental restructuring of the economy brought about by World War II, and a switch from a peacetime to a military economy, that the nation pulled out of the Great Depression.[4]

Today, economic thought embraces elements of classical, socialist, Darwinian, and Keynesian philosophy. Some economists feel that more government oversight of the economy and intervention in economic activity is desirable. Others feel that less government involvement is the best approach. To predict the effect of economic policy, economists have developed complex mathematical models, called *econometric models*, that

---

4. Some economists feel that it was not until the end of World War II, when the government relaxed wage and price controls and other New Deal restrictions on business, that the United States pulled out of the Great Depression.

through the use of computers and a variety of statistical and other analytical techniques attempt to isolate economic variables and to determine what happens when one or another variable is changed.

How well our econometric models work and how well our economic theories predict economic behavior are debatable. What is clear is that our economic practices and philosophy have changed over time, which returns us to the point with which we began the chapter. In light of our discussion on economic progress, we recognize something striking about this advance—an observation that throughout the book, and in all matters that pertain to politics, economics, and current affairs, we will find useful to keep in our thoughts. We discern a line of evolutionary ascent, a trend in the course of our economic development.

As, over the millennia, the individual evolved to greater consciousness and substance of character, society evolved from more to less collective forms. A settlement represents a less collective form of social structure than a nomadic community represents. A city-state represents a less collective social form than a settlement represents. An empire represents a less collective social form than a city-state represents, and a nation represents a less collective social form than an empire represents. Corresponding to this trend in the advance of social organization, our economic systems and ideologies evolved in support. With beginnings in the human move from a hunting and gathering way of life to an urban way of life and with setbacks and thresholds along the way, economic systems and economic thought advanced from models and philosophies that embraced a high degree of government, or other centralized form of control, and little individual freedom to forms and philosophies that embraced less government, or other centralized form of control, and greater individual freedom. A thousand years ago, a man born a peasant, had little opportunity in life other than to work the fields owned by his seigneur and to pass his servitude to his children. Today, a person born into the developed world has many educational and other opportunities. Humanity has evolved to increasingly respect the freedom and autonomy of the individual, and our economic theories and practices have reflected this development. *Figure 4* illustrates this economic trend.

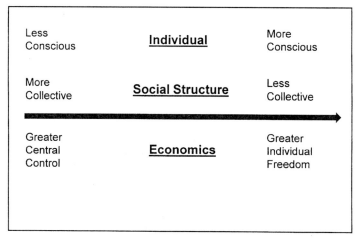

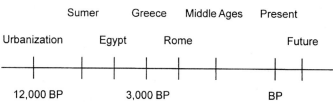

Fig. 4. Economic Trend. As human society evolved from more to less collective forms, our economic theories and practices changed to reflect this progress. We advanced from economic forms with greater central control and less individual freedom to forms with less central control and greater individual freedom.

The creative process and humanity's ascent to greater consciousness and understanding gave rise to greater autonomy and individuality. Our greater autonomy and individuality allowed us to form stronger, more intimate social bonds and less communal and more nestled and interwoven societies. As social structure became less collective, economic systems and economic thought evolved to accommodate this development. Increasingly, economic ideals and practices centered on addressing the needs and aspirations of the individual.

4

Socialism and Capitalism

IT GOES WITHOUT SAYING that today's global economy is complex. There are local, state, and national levels. There are trade alliances between nations. There are multinational corporations that function beyond the jurisdiction of any one nation. In every country, there is a governing body, an enforcing body, and a working body, but the distinction between these groups is not as clear as in the past. Less people are employed in agriculture, construction, and manufacturing and more people are employed in law, finance, accounting, and government. Often, more human resources are devoted to tracking the flow of money than to producing tangible goods and services. As we have established, all contemporary systems of economic practice are based on the assumptions that resources are by nature limited and human material wants are by nature unlimited. As such, supply and demand are central to economic function. We, however, can balance these variables in different ways. Present-day economics is dominated by two systems of allocation and production: *socialism*, which has its theoretical roots in Marxism, and *capitalism*, which has its theoretical roots in laissez-faire, classical, and Keynesian economics.

To understand how these systems work, we begin with a fundamental but often overlooked point. At the heart of any economic practice—modern, primitive, socialistic, capitalistic, or as we will see economics of fulfillment—is one factor, human creativity. Every economy exists as a result of our work, our energy, our dreams, our ambition, our skill, our drive, our knowledge, our desire to do something better or different. What other than human creativity can underlie economic activity? Though we often take the point for granted, the human ability to create is at the core of our subsistence, at the heart of all things economic.

Moreover, human creativity takes place within the individual. Corporations do not invent products. Individuals who work for corpora-

30

tions invent products. Government does not provide services. Individuals who work for government provide services. Machines may produce cars, appliances, and circuit boards, but people design, build, and maintain the machines. We may choose to align our creative efforts with others, but they are still our creative efforts. Human creativity is unique to us all. The more opportunity we as individuals have to creatively express ourselves, and thus to engage in economic activity, the more productive the economy.

The individual's creativity, in turn, is motivated by need. Our motivation may be basic, to provide the necessities of life for our families and ourselves. For most in the industrial world, our subsistence needs are not too difficult to meet, and we perceive other needs as essential to our survival and wellbeing. Some of us work to accumulate wealth, to see the balance in our bank account go up each month. Some of us work to purchase the trappings that display our wealth: a new car, a bigger house, a closet full of clothes, a higher-definition plasma television set. Some of us work for the praise of our boss and the respect of our peers, to occupy a place in the social structure provided by our employer and to advance in that structure. Some of us are driven by our passion, by the conviction that we are meant to do what we do and that we must direct our creative energy to that end. Moreover, our motivation is rarely singular. At one moment we may be driven to earn a paycheck, at another to furthering our advancement on the job, and at still another to pursuing our calling in life. Human ambition is diverse and interwoven.

No matter our motivation, for us to express our creative energy and contribute to the economy, one other factor must come into play, and in light of previous chapters it will come as no surprise. For the human being to creatively express his or herself and participate in the economy, he or she must have freedom. To produce, we must have resources and opportunity. We must have the room we need to grow and learn and to express our achievement.

Now, let us see how our assumptions of scarcity and unlimited human want and our notions of freedom, creativity, motivation, and individuality come into play in today's global economy. We begin with a look at the most basic of the global economy's dominant economic systems, socialism.

In its theoretically pure form, socialism is grounded in the notion that we can best develop and allocate scarce resources by communal regulation of the means to produce and distribute wealth. In the socialist scheme, the individual creates goods and services in accordance with the governmentally determined needs of the community. The individual then turns over the wealth he or she produces to the community, which gives back what it feels the individual needs to subsist and continue to produce. Economic needs are accessed, economic activities are planned, and economic resources are allocated through central control.

One might think that in a planned economy, it would be easy to meet everyone's needs. The government or some regulatory body simply mandates what to produce and how it should be distributed. This has not proven to be the case, and for a fundamental reason.

The socialist model assumes that the overriding human motivation is social conformity. In a socialist economy, we exist to fill a role in the state. We survive to occupy a niche in the economic machine of society. As such, the socialist model disregards all other forms of human motivation. We have no subsistence needs. At least in theory, the economy allocates what we require to support ourselves to the extent that we can further contribute to the economy. Moreover, any higher needs are disregarded. Those who administer the economy assume that we are driven by no calling other than to do what is expected of us on the job and thus to fulfill our role in society.

When we as individuals have no outlet to express any drive other than the need we feel for social conformity, our motivation is limited. Correspondingly, our creativity and the economic output that results are limited. We have all met or been that bureaucrat who takes his or her break at the same time every day and who does nothing more than what is in his or her job description. How motivated would we be at work if we were forced to give the government our paycheck and, no matter how much or little effort we put into the job and no matter how much or little money we earned, it gave back only the amount it felt we needed to buy food, pay rent, and catch the bus to work? Socialism disregards our individual need to grow and learn—our drive to build a better life for ourselves and our families, our desire to make our job our own by inventing a better way to do it. The socialist model subverts our individuality to further a presumed collective good. As such, it limits freedom and individual initiative and restricts the creative activity an economy must have to produce the goods and services its members want and require.

Consequently, and as history has graphically demonstrated, socialist governments are forced to demand social conformity and economic output. The leaders of the Soviet Union imposed strict quotas on the output of farms and factories, and workers and managers who failed to meet these quotas were often dealt with brutally. To maintain the stability and output of the state, Stalin in the Soviet Union executed an estimated forty million dissidents. In China's communist revolution, Mao Zedong executed an estimated sixty million dissidents. Socialism is central control. In an ideologically driven socialist society, rulers go to extreme lengths to maintain that control.

Even in the most oppressive economy, however, the spirit of the individual will come through. What socialist nation exists without a black market? The collective farms of the former Soviet Union were vast, but a disproportionate share of the nation's food was produced on tiny plots workers cultivated for themselves. In the 1980s, China's leaders realized that communism could not survive in a rigidly controlled form and, faced with social unrest among the population, opened their economy to business and outside investment. As the failure of the Soviet Union and the decline of Cuba, North Korea, and other predominately socialistic nations make clear, with no incentive to contribute to the economy other than political conformity, no matter how harshly it may be imposed, economic activity will invariably wind down and, as China's rulers hope to prevent, in the end collapse.

Economic systems evolved from forms with a great deal of central control and little individual freedom to forms with less central control and greater individual freedom. Evolution, however, does not take place without ups-and-downs. Marx correctly assessed the economic problems of his day and was well intended in his goal to rectify them. However noble his motivation, the communalistic scheme he came up with to achieve this end is a throwback to an earlier evolutionary era, a variant on the rigidly controlled social orders of the past. Many equate socialism with the sixties-era concept of the ecosystem, a mechanical interpretation of nature where every species has its niche and interacts to create a whole in an idealized state of balance. In this vein, there are those who today call for socialism. Most that do, however, have no real understanding of economic evolution and no accurate concept of what socialism is and how it works. More to the point, they see the power of central control vested in themselves.

By its nature, socialism is a limited economic philosophy. As such, few of us encounter it in a form that approaches its theoretical ideal. Rather, we see it in taxpayer funded entitlements and social services. In this sense, every country employs a blend of free market and centrally controlled economic practices—a modern incarnation of the play between economic approaches established when humankind moved from a hunting and gathering way of life to an urban way of life. Some nations, as France and Germany, lean toward a planned economy. Others, as Taiwan and the United States, lean toward a market-driven economy. This brings us to the chapter's next objective. To whatever extent a nation may implement taxpayer-funded services and programs, socialism cannot exist without a degree of capitalism.

Whereas socialism embodies no motivation to produce other than social conformity, the motivation expressed by a member of a capitalist economy is more diverse. That, however, is not to say that capitalism is without its limitations. As varied as the individual's needs and desires may be under capitalism, they, as under socialism, are fundamentally materialistic.

The capitalist approach centers on the idea that we can best achieve our economic ends by letting our needs directly dictate economic activity—by the *market*. In capitalism, the overriding motivation to produce and contribute to the economy is *profit*: the ability to get more out of an economic activity than we put into it, measured in dollars. Driven by the need for profit, we create or identify markets and supply goods and services targeted to those markets. Our needs, choices, and desires drive economic activity, and those that profit from this activity do what they can to address and for their benefit influence our needs, choices, and desires.

This directs our discussion to the idea of capital. Textbooks define capital as the body of goods and moneys from which we derive wealth, or a bigger body of goods and moneys. But capital means something more—opportunity. In a capitalist economy, control over capital gives the individual the means to raise a family, start a business, earn an education, or in some way transform their motivation, as diverse as it may be expressed, into creative activity and contribute to the economy. The flaw of capitalism, of course, is that not everyone has access to capital and thus to the freedom and opportunity to fully exercise their creative power.

To understand this, we need to peel away the layers of economic theory and look at the mechanism of capitalism, in particular at something called the *capital cycle*.

Say we have 100 thousand dollars and invest our money by building a house. When finished, our house includes 50 thousand dollars of labor and 50 thousand dollars of land and materials. Now, say, due to favorable market conditions we sell our house for 150 thousand dollars. By virtue of the relationship between supply and demand—or cost and what people are willing to pay—we turn a 50 thousand dollar profit.

But there is more to capitalism than revenues minus expenses. We made money, but where did our profit, the extra fifty thousand dollars, come from? The difference between what we put into the economy and what we got out of the economy came from a transfer of wealth within the economy. We ended up with fifty thousand dollars more capital, and the economy, excluding ourselves, ended up with fifty thousand dollars less capital. Factors such as money supply, inflation, deflation, and the value added by our management and the reshaping of raw materials into a finished product influence this situation, but they do not change the mechanism. We now have more resources, and thus freedom and opportunity to creatively express ourselves and contribute to society and the economy, and everyone else has less.

As this process repeats, capital concentrates in the hands of fewer and fewer individuals. We have the situation Marx grappled with more than a century ago and we see throughout the world today: The rich get richer, and the poor get poorer. Wealth concentration is not a function of greed and human failing, though greed and human failing may come into play. It is an intrinsic, inescapable characteristic of a profit-driven market economy.

Because of the mathematical certitude with which wealth will concentrate in a profit-driven market economy, a mechanism must exist to redistribute capital. Beneath all its layers of legal, political, accounting, and regulatory complexity, capitalism is nothing more than a scheme to create opportunity and thus economic activity by capital redistribution. Capitalism is a system that over the last several centuries has evolved to cycle wealth from areas where it has accumulated to areas where it can be put to work—the capital cycle.

In this pursuit, and as *Figure 5* shows, economies employ a variety of techniques to redistribute capital, or to manage the flow of the capital cycle. The most important are a nation's banking system and its bond, stock, and other exchanges. By the promise of shared profits, banks and exchanges give the individual access to the money needed to start a business, earn an education, develop an invention, or in some way play a role in the economy. To a lesser extent, nations provide capital through tax or charity funded social programs: welfare, unemployment, and other social services.

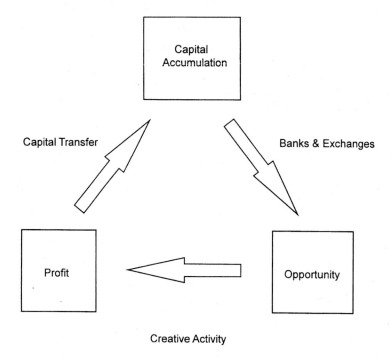

Fig. 5. Capital Cycle. Capital accumulation is not a consequence of greed and human failing, though greed and human failing may come into play. It is an inescapable aspect of a profit driven, free market economy. Capitalism is a system that cycles capital from areas where it has accumulated to areas where it can be put to work.

The better a nation or economy's mechanisms of capital redistribution, and thus the greater the opportunity the average individual has to direct his or her motivation to a creative effort and as a consequence to play a role in the economy and to put its available capital to use, the better the economy works—the less the pie is divided up and the more the pie increases in size.

But as anyone who has started a business knows, money can be hard to come by. Due to a natural reluctance to put investment funds at risk, a nation or economy's mechanisms of capital redistribution are not available to all or, to be realistic with regard to investment, to most members of the economy. This creates an economy that, as Keynes and others sought to understand, operates unevenly, that has booms and recessions.

Many factors, tangible and psychological, come into play in the pattern of economic ups-and-downs that we call the business cycle, but its root cause may not be as complex as Keynes thought and most economists today believe.

Economic activity shows a direct relationship to the level of creative activity generated by the individual. Creative activity, in turn, shows a direct relationship to the level of opportunity we as individuals have to channel our motivation to a creative endeavor. The greater the level of opportunity we experience, the greater the degree and originality of our creative efforts, the more the goods and services that result, and the better the economy works.

The level of opportunity we experience, in turn, shows a direct relationship to the level of investment capital available to us as individuals. The less control over capital we enjoy, the less freedom we experience to live and work to our potential—the less opportunity we have to start a business, pay for college, perfect an invention, or in some way contribute to the economy.

As capital concentrates, opportunity decreases and economic activity winds down. Ultimately, the economy faces a period of restructuring and, at least in the minds of most but by no means all economists and politicians, the need for investment and consumer stimulation to redistribute capital before things pick up and the process repeats. Whereas if left alone a socialist economy will in the end fail, a capitalist economy will demonstrate the booms-and-busts of the business cycle—perhaps better characterized as the *opportunity cycle*.

This, of course, brings us to a question dear to the heart of every economist and politician. How can we better redistribute capital and smooth out the booms-and-busts of the opportunity cycle? Classical, or laissez-faire, economists believe that this happens best when we don't do anything—that the economy will self-regulate to full employment and optimal production and distribution. Most economists, however, think that the economy requires some oversight, some regulatory management.

To develop this point and better understand our inability to manage the economy without the booms and busts of the opportunity cycle, we must move past socialism and capitalism in their theoretically pure forms and look at the spectrum of economic practices that every nation employs. As *Figure 6* shows, on one theoretical extreme, we find Marxist socialism and absolute central control. On the other theoretical extreme, we find unregulated free markets and a complete absence of central control. If our economic practices lean too far toward either end of the central control and free market spectrum, we impede the capital redistribution cycle. Individual opportunity decreases, and the economy, or as is more frequently the case today a segment of the economy, winds down.

Fig. 6. Socialist-Capitalist Spectrum. Today's scarcity-based economic systems embody a spectrum of economic practices. On one theoretical extreme, we find socialism and absolute central control. On the other theoretical extreme, we find unregulated free markets and a complete absence of central control. If our economic practices lean too far toward either end of the central control and free market spectrum, we impede the capital redistribution cycle. Individual opportunity decreases, and the economy, or as is more frequently the case today a segment of the economy, winds down

In the state of California during the first years of this century, for example, socialistic policies of extreme taxation and environmental and other regulation created an economic climate so inhospitable to investment that a shrinking private sector could not support a growing public sector and the state government faced insolvency. Interestingly, the situation was compounded by an absence of central control on the part of the federal government. Free trade and labor policies drove jobs and investment to India, Mexico, Indonesia, and other low wage, low regulation countries devastating the state's technology, agriculture, and manufacturing industries.

As this point illustrates, unrestricted market activity also impedes capital redistribution. Free from all oversight, a profit-driven market economy will produce monopolistic concentrations of capital—rich and poor nations and as we see in the developing world and are beginning to see in the United States and other developed nations—a tiered economy. We create an economy with a small rich segment where capital and opportunity are available and the economy works, a shrinking middle class where capital and opportunity are limited and the standard of living is declining, and a growing poor segment where capital and opportunity are almost nonexistent and poverty is rampant. This is why one statistic tells us that the economy is growing, or as of recently poised for a recovery, and another that living standards are declining and family-wage jobs are disappearing. The economy's upper tier is so productive that it offsets declining economic activity on lower tiers. When one politician says that the economy is structurally sound and another that it is the worst since the Great Depression both are telling, or avoiding, the truth. It is a matter of how we gather and interpret the statistics.

We also create dominant corporations and another limit to our creative freedom—*corporate socialism*. The IBMs, Nike's, and Walmarts of the world thrive in an economic environment where they are free to buy or produce for a low cost in a deflated third-world economy and sell for a high price in an inflated industrial economy. Yet, internally, these and nearly all corporations function through rigid central control. From the standpoint of the individual and our individual need for creative expression, what is the difference between working in the economic machine of the corporation or in the economic machine of the state? Given the tendency of businesses and other organizations to stagnate and become bureaucratic, what does this tell us about the periods of corporate downsizing and restructuring we experience, not to mention the ultimate future of today's multinational corporation?

To narrow our discussion to economic theory, when we look at the balance between central control and free market governance, we see that to function properly the capital cycle must operate within some form of centrally established, or governmentally administered, business environment. Difficulty arises when—through over regulation, under regulation, or regulation that benefits one interest at the expense of others—government fails to structure this business environment in a way that optimizes the flow of capital and creates economic opportunity.

In this regard, we can impede the capital cycle at two critical points: the level of the borrower and the level of the lender. From the standpoint of the borrower, when we impede the capital cycle, we, through our regulatory structure, make it hard to open or expand a business or to in a tangible way contribute to the economy—high taxes, excessive environmental regulation, politically motivated subsidies that benefit one industry at the expense of another. From the standpoint of the lender, when we impede the capital cycle, we make it difficult for an investor to receive a reasonable rate of return at a reasonable risk. We create policies that reward risky lending or, conversely, that reward excessively restrictive lending. We create policies that encourage investment in companies that jiggle money around rather than produce tangible goods and services.

The consequences are twofold: first, we slow down the flow of capital. This results in a downturn in the economy or in a segment of the economy. Capital, however, has to go somewhere. Second, we create a capital bubble. When investors do not have the option to at a reasonable level of risk and return invest in companies that produce tangible goods and services, they buy and sell speculating on price. We make money off of money, gamble that whatever asset or security we are investing in today will, by virtue of the speculation of others, be worth more when we sell it tomorrow. Speculation itself is not the culprit. When we think gas is going up in price, we speculate, take a chance and fill up today instead of tomorrow. The problem lies is the circumstances in which we speculate. When we bottleneck the capital cycle, we create a pool of paper capital, artificial wealth. And, like a plugged artery the leads to a fatal aneurism, when the speculation that drove the price of the stocks, currency, real estate, or whatever asset we are buying drives up the price too far above the asset's real worth, the bubble bursts.

But there is more to establishing a coherent economic environment and optimizing the flow of capital than laws and administrative guidelines. To further combat the ups-and-downs of the business cycle and the bottlenecks and bubbles that develop in the flow of capital, government has made available two immediate, though rather blunt, tools to intervene in the economy, or to manage the flow of the capital cycle: *fiscal* and *monetary* policy.

In the United States, monetary policy is set by a system of private banks called the Federal Reserve, or the *Fed*, and similar central banking systems exist in other nations and in the European Union. By buying and selling government securities, by changing the *reserve ratio*, or the percentage of deposits banks must keep at a Reserve Bank, by changing the *discount rate*, or the interest rate charged to banks for borrowing from a Reserve Bank, and by other recently implemented techniques such as buying none-government backed securities, the Fed regulates the amount of money in the economy. The more money, the easier it is to raise capital.

But if there is too much money in the economy, each dollar will be worth less and prices will go up—*inflation.*

Government directly intervenes in the economy with fiscal, or tax and spending, policy. *Demand-side* economists and politicians, exemplified by United States Presidents Lyndon Johnson, Jimmy Carter, and Barack Obama think the best way to grow the economy is to direct tax revenue to low and middle-income people, increasing their ability to buy and encouraging businesses to expand and hire to meet demand. *Supply-side* economists and politicians, exemplified by President Ronald Reagan, *reaganomics,* think the best way to grow the economy is to make tax revenue available for investment, or as did Reagan and in earlier and later presidencies, John F. Kennedy and George W. Bush, to cut taxes, encouraging businesses to start and to create jobs thus giving people more money to spend.

As this debate goes around and around, so do the booms and busts of the business cycle. When the economy is doing great, leaders take credit. When it is doing badly, they blame their predecessors. Though arguably sound in theory, in practice fiscal and monetary policy and demand and supply-side economic policies have not proven to be particularly effective management tools.

If economic activity winds down when our economic practices shift too far to either end of the central control and free market spectrum, the key to establishing the business environment needed to expedite capital flow would be to maintain the correct level of central control, the right blend of market activity and government oversight. In theory, we can accomplish this through appropriate and not excessive taxation, through appropriate and not excessive regulation, through coherent management of imports and exports, through reforming the banking and exchange systems to put ease and flexibility of capital redistribution before profit and speculation, and through limiting the size to which a company can grow and force out competition. Economic activity rests on the creativity of the individual. No matter the outward manifestation of an economic downturn—recession or depression, a slowdown in a segment of the economy or a slowdown in the economy as a whole—to get the economy moving, we must create the business environment where the creativity of the individual can unfold.

As the world's economic ups-and-downs and the widening gap between rich and poor nations and classes makes clear, however, no government has for any substantial period of time struck the right balance between free markets and the regulatory structure in which they operate. Arguably, the closest a government has come was the economic boom experienced by the United States from the end of World War II to the mid-1970s. Not only did America prosper during this time, its economic growth and stability fueled the rebuilding of Japan and Europe, a never-before-seen period of economic expansion. As memorable as it was, the conditions that made this period of economic prosperity possible were more a factor of technology and of a global shift from a war to a peace-time economy than of government policy—though a relaxation of wage, price, and other controls imposed during the Great Depression contrib-uted to the period's prosperity. Can the socialist-capitalist framework of today fuel a similar explosion of economic activity and more importantly sustain such prosperity?

At one time, economic activities took place largely within a nation's legal boundaries. As such, the flow of capital could be regulated to the degree allowed by political concerns. Today, capital changes hands with little regard to political or geographical divisions. In our global economy, economic activities take place subject to the regulatory requirements of many nations and governing bodies. To manage capital flow on a global scale, we would need some form of planet-wide regulatory structure, some form of world government. Is this realistic? Is this desirable? Is this what is underlying controversial developments such as free trade zones, open border policies, the European Union, the future North American Union, the expanded power of the United Nations and World Bank, and increasingly frequent calls to replace national currencies with a single, world currency?

As important, throughout most of history there was land and other non-monetary forms of capital available—the frontier. Today, virtu-ally every resource has a monetary value. We equate capital strictly with money. There is no West to pioneer, no land to homestead, no resources available to the average individual not accounted for on some corporate or government ledger.

Moreover, risk factors and political interests limit the availability of capital to favored economic segments. A multinational corporation may have no problem raising the money to open a factory or to build a chain of stores or restaurants. If a family who wants to start a small business can get a loan at all, they may have to secure it with their home. Similarly, the economies of scale a highly capitalized firm enjoys make it difficult for a small business to compete. How many independent clothing makers and designers does a chain of department stores prevent from going into business? Banks are not in business to redistribute capital but to make money redistributing capital. Their motivation is to maximize return and to minimize the risk of loss. Similarly, stock, commodity, and other exchanges have in the minds of many deteriorated into gambling arenas where a select few with control over vast amounts of capital speculate while workers pay the cost of market instability and investor psychology. In effect, those who control the capital function as the gatekeepers of the economy. For profit or other motivation, they determine who will receive investment funds and for what purpose. In the 1950s, almost anyone in the United States with skill and ambition could start a small business. Today, the cost and plethora of regulations the entrepreneur faces demand a high degree of capitalization and legal and accounting savvy.

Socialistic methods of wealth redistribution have proven even less effective. Welfare and other entitlements make so little capital available to the average individual that they do almost nothing to create economic opportunity. A person on the dole may have the money to buy groceries but not the money to open a grocery store. Moreover, excessive socialistic wealth redistribution, as when taxes are high, draws funds out of the capital redistribution cycle, diluting capital to the point where it becomes harder to pool enough to invest. Economic activity declines. Unemployment and the demand for social services increases, as does government's call for still higher taxes to pay for them. Social programs keep people afloat, stabilize demand forces, and maintain the social stability necessary for a market economy to function but in a fundamental way do little to fuel economic activity and create wealth.

The issue of capital redistribution through taxation illustrates a widely held misconception about how a government budget works. Most of us and most of our leaders see the economy as static. We think of the federal or other government budget as a checkbook. If we raise tax rates, the government has more money to spend. If we lower tax rates, the government has less money to spend. But a market economy is not static; it functions through the flow of capital. Taxes are collected on economic activity: on payment of a salary, purchase of a product, assessment of a property value. As such, the greater the number of transactions and the greater their dollar amount, the more tax revenue collected. When the economy grows and more money changes hands, tax revenues go up. When the economy shrinks and less money changes hands, tax revenues go down. If we raise tax rates too high and draw too much money out of the capital cycle, we limit investment. Economic activity slows down, and tax revenues decrease. In the United States, it is widely accepted that President Kennedy's tax rate cuts in the 1960s, which dropped the top tax rate from in the low ninety percents to just above seventy percent, sustained the post World War II economic boom, which had begun to decline, into the early 1970s. Similarly, tax revenues by some measures nearly doubled following President Reagan's tax rate cuts in the 1980s, which dropped the top tax rate from the seventy percents to below thirty percent. In the Reagan years, the often criticized budget deficit would, by most assessments, have been far worse had tax cuts not gone into effect. Many feel that George W. Bush's tax cuts also boosted the economy, though it is harder to say because they were comparatively small. Tax revenues in the years that immediately followed, however, exceeded the amount critics of the Bush tax cuts predicted.

On the expense side, balancing the federal budget is also not the same as balancing our checkbook. Some government expenses drain the coffers. Others boost the economy and increase tax revenues. In the United States, do we need to subsidize the relocation of manufacturing firms oversees? Do we need to fund a study on the racial or sexual stereotypes of college-age males living in fraternity houses, an example that typifies much of government funded research in the humanities and social sciences. Do we need to subsidize the production of corn-based ethanol, a move that has fueled a massive increase in the cost of grain and that in many parts of the world has contributed to hunger and spurred riots and political instability? Often to the point of absurdity, much of what government spends provides no tangible benefit to society or the economy. It merely takes wealth from one group of people and gives it to another. As Ronald Reagan described it, every dollar the government gives someone it takes from someone else. In contrast, the massive irrigation, hydroelectric, and other public works projects of the 1930s, World War II, the GI Bill of Rights or Servicemen's Readjustment Act of 1944, the 1948 Marshal Plan to rebuild Europe, and the interstate highway system of the 1950s and 1960s have fueled growth and paid for themselves many times over. The government maximizes revenues when the economy does best. From a strictly economic standpoint, sound public policy directs government resources to activities that offset the drag of taxation.

In part, our failure to strike a balance between market forces and central control rests with the politics of government. A decision made to benefit the economy as a whole will invariably be to the determent of one or more political factions, compelling leaders to base economic policy on the influence of the powerful interests that fund their political ambitions. Environmental, public employee lobbies, and the demand-side economists they employ fight to shift policy toward the central control end of the spectrum. Corporations, entrepreneurs, small business owners, and the supply-side economists they employ fight to shift policy toward the free market end.

But there is more to it than politics and the struggle for power. Economists have long grasped the relationship between central control and free market economic behavior. Capitalism, it is understood, cannot function without a degree of socialism. Socialism, it is understood, cannot function without a substantial allotment of capitalism. There are economists and politicians who argue that the blend should lean one way or the other, but most agree that some level of balance is necessary. Capitalism may be the driving force behind economic growth, but to function it needs some form of overall regulatory structure. Why, then, do nations seem unable to maintain the right degree of slant, and why at this point in history does doing so seem particularly out of our reach?

Across the spectrum of economic implementation, our adherence to contemporary economic theories and practices has locked the individual into an ever more invasive monetary economy. Today's global economy is a machine with a life of its own, and we are a cog in the works. Pundits and economists reduce the value of the human being to a statistic: to an unemployment number, to a measure of productivity, purchasing power, and consumer confidence. We are a source of demand, a commodity in a labor market, a variable quantified and manipulated in an econometric model. Every aspect of our lives is valued, tracked, and accounted for. There are those who call for a global economy free of national borders, but they do not understand the concept of collectivity and the evolution of human social structure to less collective forms. The economy on the level of the community establishes the basis for the economy on the level of the city, which establishes the basis for the economy on the level of the state. We can create a global economy, but to be stable it cannot be imposed from the top down. It must function through strong national economies, which function through strong state economies, which function through strong economies on successively lower levels.

As disturbing, we embrace contemporary economic theories and practices with unquestioning devotion. Faced with problems under socialism, we grope for solutions in capitalism and free markets. Faced with problems under capitalism, we grope for solutions in socialism and central control. When have we questioned the assumptions of scarcity and unlimited human want? Given our materialistic view of the world, what pundit or economist on the political right has challenged the validity of competition and economic Darwinism? What pundit or economist on the political left has challenged the validity of central control and the need for government regulation? To us, today, economics is a dogma, an ideology, a religion. Whereas in earlier times, and in particular in the hunting and gathering society, the economy existed to serve our needs, we exist to serve the ideology and mechanism of the economy. Though we may cringe at the thought and deny our subservience, most of us have accepted and grown content with the challenge our economic ideals pose to our humanity. We bow before the altar of the global economic machine. Our economic doctrine does not serve us; we slave to the false profit of our economic doctrine.

As such, our economic theories and practices restrict the action on which all economic activity is fundamentally based, the creative initiative of the individual. Increasingly, we devote our creative efforts to managing the flow of money—and to the legal and political manipulation that allows us to do so to our advantage—rather than to producing tangible goods and services. Increasingly, the world's exchanges and banking systems are driven by speculation. Money is made off of money and concentrated in the hands of a few, while leaders struggle to keep the global economy from unraveling as each speculative bubble bursts. We weather declining middle class living standards and increasing poverty. We weather banking scandals, energy scandals, accounting scandals, real estate scandals—the rise and collapse of this or that market, the strength and weakness of this or that currency.

Politicians and economists cannot achieve the right blend of socialistic and capitalistic economic practices because such is not obtainable. Economics as we know it is obsolete, sustained by our stagnation—held past its time by our complacency. Scarcity-based economics has brought

46

us to where we are at and over the centuries has dramatically elevated the human condition but cannot meet the demands of the beings we are becoming. Economic practices based on the assumptions of limited natural resources and unlimited human wants—reinforced by Darwinian ideals of competition and survival of the fittest and Marxist ideals of egalitarianism and of "for the collective good"—are to an ever-greater extent unable to meet our needs and expectations. We, as human beings, have and will continue to evolve. We, as human beings, have and will continue to demand economic models that provide greater individual freedom, greater choice and opportunity. Socialism and capitalism are outmoded, past their day, relics of history destined for evolution's trailing arrow. The economic turmoil embodied in today's global economy—the economic failings, and the consequences of suffering and social conflict, that every day we read about in the paper and hear about on the news—is the symptom of obsolescence, the manifestation of the uncertainty of transformation that masses within the human community. The bottom line, as humanity crosses the universe's threshold to meaning, the socialistic and capitalistic economic ideologies that developed during the evolutionary period we call understanding can no longer meet our material or our spiritual needs.[1]

With this recognition, we take the first step toward a new economic reality. Today, we witness economic hardship around the world and its social and military consequences and ask how much can the human spirit endure. We also understand that change takes place through the creative process. The uncertainty that today tightens its grip on the planet must collapse, and at the moment it does our future will become clear. With our recognition of this, we take the first step into a new evolutionary period. We cross the threshold to meaning and, so enlightened, setout to create a new way of economic life: to mold an economics for the human beings that we have and will continue to become, to fashion an economics for the future that we see taking shape before us—an economics for the universe's age of fulfillment. The millennia-old trend in human social evolution from the collective and the centrally controlled to the less collective and the free continues. Marx was correct; capitalism is a transitional system. The economic philosophy to replace it, however, will have little in common with any Marx envisioned.

1. See *Book 1, Evolution of Consciousness*, chapter 13.

PART TWO

Economics of Fulfillment

5

Assumptions and Guiding Principle

IN THIS SECTION OF the book, we build on our knowledge of past and contemporary economic theories and practices to outline the economic theories and practices of tomorrow—the economic values and mechanisms that the evolutionary trend from the collective and the controlled to the less collective and the free and individualistic leads us to conclude is poised to unfold. I call this system of economic beliefs *economics of fulfillment*. We identify the assumptions on which our economic philosophy is based and from these assumptions derive the guiding principle to which it must aspire. With this philosophical base established, we develop a system of economic activity designed to function under the economics of fulfillment blanket and explore the real-world feasibility of our system.

Any conceptual edifice rests on assumptions. Darwinian natural selection is based on the assumptions that mutations randomly occur in organism structure, that they weaken or strengthen the organism, and that the environment selects for these mutations. Contemporary economic theory is based on the assumptions of scarcity and unlimited human wants. As we described in *Threshold to Meaning: Book 1, Evolution of Consciousness*, the theory of the creative process is based on certain fundamental definitions: emptiness, fulfillment, object, and perception.[1] These definitions are so simple and ring-true on such a basic level that we deem them reasonable. They strike us as self-evident. We accept them as representative of reality and for this reason have confidence that the vision of evolution they allow to unfold is also representative of reality. Our economics of fulfillment philosophy also rests on assumptions, and they are an outgrowth of the larger evolution of consciousness view. In this chapter, we highlight our economic philosophy's key suppositions.

1. See *Book 1, Evolution of Consciousness*, chapters 1 and 2.

Because they are a derivative of a larger philosophical perspective, for their contextual development and philosophical justification I refer you to the earlier book.

As we have established, at the heart any economic system is one factor: human creativity. It is the drive, productivity, and inventiveness of the individual. Economics of fulfillment takes this aspect of economic function to be paramount. As such, the first assumption on which we base the economic philosophy of tomorrow is, as in the evolution of consciousness view it can only be, the notion of *intrinsic human worth*.

In contrast, today's scarcity-based economic ideologies embrace a Darwinian ideal of the human being, inspired by the human move to an urban way of life. To the Darwinian trained natural and social scientist of today, we are a species like any other, swept along in a torrent of competition, the occupant of a niche in the works of the biosphere. The human being is not seen as part of a greater evolution, as on evolution's "leading edge." We as a species have no value other than as a biological entity adrift in the random turns of natural selection.

Corresponding to this view of ourselves, today's economy is a vast mechanism. As we described in Chapter 4, *Socialism and Capitalism*, in the interaction between the economy and the human being, the economy is supreme. Whether socialistic or capitalistic, the economy does not serve us. We are a component in the economic works. Our place in the economy is as a consumer, the occupant of a job title, a number on an entitlement form, an element in the production process. Businesses compete for customers. We compete to work and to make the money we need to sustain our existence. Today's economy reduces our human essence to a quantification of our existing and potential economic value. The economic machine does not serve us. We serve the economic machine.

As a result, our lives are subject to the whims of the economy. The media reports interest rates, corporate mergers, and stock markets trends. Commentators argue about taxes, budgets, fiscal and monetary policy, classical and Keynesian economics. The media also reports layoffs. On occasion, it even reports the consequences of layoffs—crime, shattered lives, and broken families. But when has the media challenged the notion of layoffs, the concept that we can put human beings aside in the name of the system's function? When has the media questioned an economic ideology that embraces doctrine over the lives of the people such doctrine should serve? When has the media looked beyond socialism and capitalism? When has the media asked us to envision a way of life where we are not subject to economic mood, where we are not subservient to investor psychology and to the uncertainty of the opportunity cycle?

In the economics of fulfillment framework, we take as a given the supremacy of the human being. No matter what economic system or systems we devise to function under the economics of fulfillment blanket, we must structure them to serve us. We must engineer our economic interaction to fulfill our material needs and our deeper human needs of creativity and personal growth. By virtue of our birth, by virtue of our place in creation, we each play a role in humankind's advance. No one can be left behind. No one is more worthy of existence and of a fulfilling life than anyone else is. Every human being is vital to our future. Humanity cannot achieve its ultimate state of being until every human being achieves his or her ultimate state of being. In our economics of fulfillment philosophy and the systems of economic activity we invent for its implementation, we can have no losers. We can have no one left behind. We take as implicit and self-evident the value of the individual. We embrace the assumption of intrinsic human worth.

The second supposition on which we base our economics of fulfillment philosophy is the notion of *abundance*. It is the assumption that physical resources exist, or by our ingenuity can be made to exist, to whatever extent we may need to meet our individual material and creative needs and by doing so to further the human endeavor on Earth. Because our assumption of abundance is in complete opposition to the assumption of scarcity that we have been taught to accept as the natural condition of the world, we need to look at it in detail.

Contemporary economics evolved out of the scarcity experienced by the early urban community. As any economic text will tell you and as we have said on more than one occasion, current economic theory rests on the notion that resources are by nature limited and human material wants are by nature unlimited. Socialism, capitalism, and their variations are schemes to encourage production and to divvy up what we produce.

On first glance, it is hard to argue with the idea of scarcity and with the need for systems like socialism and capitalism to accommodate it. The Earth is only so big. Raw materials therefore must be limited. There is only so much iron, nickel, copper, silicon, aluminum, and other minerals close enough to the surface of Earth's crust for us to get our hands on. But when we look deeper, the idea of limited resources is not as self-evident as it may seem.

Limits exist in nature. This we cannot dispute. There is only so much oil in the world. There is only so much land suitable for agriculture. There are only so many rivers that we can harness for irrigation. But a physical limit by itself has no meaning. The notion of scarce resources exists only in light of our demand for those resources. If we assume raw materials are inherently limited, we are forced to accept the second part of our textbook definition of economic suppositions. We must also assume that human material wants are unlimited, that the human need for material wealth is unbounded. Our material craving is insatiable.

Common sense, of course, tells us that this is not the case. To say that our material need is unlimited is to say that our motivation is no more than material. Love, peace of mind, the elation we feel after we break through to a new level of consciousness and understanding, these and other needs have no bearing in the economic realm. We cannot fulfill them through economic power and material acquisition. We create satisfaction in life and further our personal evolution in many ways. But not every desire has a physical basis or resolution.

The idea of unlimited material need is a product of nineteenth and twentieth century reasoning. The economist who says we are driven by the need to survive and therefore our physical needs must be unlimited speaks with the same voice as the physicist who says we cannot measure the extent of the cosmos therefore space must be infinite or since energy is conserved the universe must have begun in a state of infinite heat and density.[2] Our want for material goods is not insatiable. The assumption that the human need for material wealth is unlimited is outmoded, a conclusion that is no longer applicable. It is not reasonable.

If we cannot justify the notion of unlimited human wants, we cannot justify the notion of scarce resources. There are limits to raw materials on the planet, but these limits exceed our potential for their use and therefore are not relevant. The assumption of limited resources and unlimited human wants embodies the contradiction that at least from the standpoint of logic and philosophy negates its validity.

But do the physical limits that exist in nature really exceed our potential for their use? We experience and read about shortages every day.

2. See *Book 1, Evolution of Consciousness*, chapter 7.

Poverty, hunger, and a lack of basic health services plague the developing world. Seemingly ever-higher prices plague the industrial nations. Many of us struggle, or have to work harder, to procure the basics of existence, and few of us have all the goods and services we need or desire. But are the unsatisfied material needs we experience the result of a shortage of raw materials and basic resources?

Take, for example, the harvest of "old-growth" timber in the Northwest United States.[3] By some measures, the timber industry in the Northwest faces a shortage of the large-diameter pine, douglas fir, and other softwood species milled into lumber and used to frame houses. Heavy logging decades ago reduced the supply and created conflict between business and environmental interests so intense that it has polarized the management of public lands and led to arson and other forms of eco-terrorism. We face a physical limit to the amount of old growth timber available for harvest in the Northwest United States, or do we?

Although by historical standards the amount of mature timber may be reduced, it does not limit the number of homes we can build. The debate as to whether there is a timber shortage at all aside, and it is a legitimate debate, we can build better homes out of reinforced concrete than out of wood—homes that can withstand fire, flood, tornadoes, and earthquakes, homes that are architecturally superior and that are easier to heat, cool, and maintain. The shortage of old growth timber is a product of the way we deal with the resource and not a limit imposed on us by nature. It is an outcome of the way the construction industry in the United States has traditionally built homes. If we were to modernize our building techniques and make houses out of concrete, our need for softwood would decrease, and there would be less demand for mature timber and no real or perceived shortage of supply.

It is of course natural to ask if there are limits to the amount of reinforced concrete we can pour. The major ingredient used to make steel rebar is iron. Iron is the fourth most plentiful element in the Earth's crust—so common that we see cars rusting on the roadside or cluttering backyards because it often costs more to haul the debris away than to refine the raw materials. The ingredients of concrete are even more plentiful. They are sand and gravel and the clay and limestone used to make portland cement. So common are these substances that we cannot

3. See *Book 3, Blueprint for Reconstruction,* chapters 2 and 4.

imagine a time when we would run out of them. Sand, gravel, clay, and limestone are ubiquitous, abundant on almost every part of the globe. Moreover, steel rebar can be recycled, and concrete, which when cured is essentially a form of sedimentary stone, can be crushed and used as aggregate for a variety of purposes, even to mix new concrete.

Another example of a scarce resource that is not scarce is food. The human community faces a devastating problem with hunger. In many nations, waves of hunger ravish the population and create intense social conflict. Even wealthy nations such as the United States cannot assure their population of an adequate food supply.

But hunger has nothing to do with a shortage of food or with limits to the potential of the Earth's biosphere to sustain human population and agricultural production. In today's economy, food is business. Production is not motivated by humanitarian need but by profit. If it makes money to produce tomatoes in a tropical nation for export to Europe or the United States, companies buy up land and produce tomatoes. Under the rules of scarcity-based economics, it does not matter if enough land is left over for the local population to feed itself.

Moreover, political forces compel farmers to take thousands of acres of agricultural land out of production to create wetlands and other conservation areas. Conversely, as population grows and communities sprawl, we pave over vast tracts of farmland. The economic value derived from the land taken out of production to create a conservation area or on which a subdivision or a shopping mall are built—the value placed on it by political and market forces—is greater than the economic value derived from the land if it were used to grow food. We need conservation areas. We also need homes and one can argue shopping malls. But we need to eat. Those who benefit from conservation areas or who live in subdivisions and patronize shopping malls may have the money to buy food grown elsewhere, but not everyone is as high on the economic pecking order. Economic values may not reflect a commodity's true value, or its value with respect to the overall human condition.[4]

Throughout history, humanity has faced supposed natural limits to resources. In the early days of the bronze age, tin and copper were rare and valuable commodities. Never could the early maker of metal spear and arrow points have envisioned the vast quantities of these metals that

4. Ibid., chapter 4.

we would one day extract from the Earth. The classical economist Thomas Robert Malthus felt that human population would always exceed food production, this at a time when the Earth's population measured in the hundreds of millions as opposed to the six or more billion that live today. Never could Malthus have imagined the potential of modern agriculture. Economic scarcity is not a function of natural limits; is it a function of human need and ingenuity with respect to natural limits.

That said, hunger, poverty, and a lack of basic health services do exist in the undeveloped world. In the developed world, we do experience price increases, and many of us do have to work harder to maintain our standard of living. Supply and demand, markets and the momentary valuation of products, do take place. Every day, we face limits to the quantities of the goods and services available to us.

Take steel and concrete, which despite an abundance of natural resources and the potential for almost unlimited production more than doubled in cost during recent years. In part, this increase was due to demand created by rapidly growing Indian and Chinese economies. In part, it was due to foreign competition driving European and United States mills and plants out of operation. In part, it was due to environmental restrictions that in certain regions have made it impossible to build steel mills and cement plants.

Similarly,[5] gasoline prices in the United States fluctuate throughout the year, often with no correlation to demand and despite fluctuations in and often dramatic increases in the price of crude oil. The reason is refining capacity. Due to environmental activism and regulations, the nation has not built a new refinery since the early 1970s. Existing refineries operate so near capacity that when for weather, accident, maintenance, an interruption of imports, or other reason—real or contrived—a plant goes offline, shortages result and prices go up.

Consider also the production of bio-fuels from food crops: in particular ethanol made from corn. Driven by the agribusiness and environmental lobbies, and sold to the American people under the guise of energy independence and to halt "global warming,"[6] politicians in that country have passed laws that mandate the production of ethanol and other bio-fuels. The cost of corn, soybeans, and sugar crops has soared,

5. Ibid., chapter 9.
6. Ibid., chapter 10.

and agricultural production has shifted from food to fuel crops. Poultry farms and feedlots have scaled back production or gone out of business because farmers cannot afford feed. Surplus crops are not available for export, and the world's most vulnerable face hunger and social upheaval. The United States consumes approximately 135 billion gallons of gasoline each year. One acre of corn produces about 50 gallons of ethanol and it takes about the same amount of energy in the form of diesel, fertilizer, and electricity to plant, harvest, and extract that ethanol. No one benefits from the production of ethanol from corn other than the farming and environmental interests that drove the policy.

The scarcity experienced by the early urban community was real. The scarcity we face is fabricated. When we have a need for a good or service and it is not affordable, and when we have a need for a job or a career and it is not attainable, our economic system fails to align demand with the ability to produce and is not working as it should. We have the knowledge to reshape our world in almost any way we imagine. Technology has rendered natural limits obsolete. Scarcity is a product of politics and economics. Socialism and capitalism are relics of another age. They rest on the notion of scarcity and cannot function without it. When scarcity does not exist, they create it.

The universe has never evolved and could never evolve to a state that precluded its continued evolution. This is not the nature of the creative process. We do not live in a world of scarce resources. From an evolution of consciousness, and thus an economics of fulfillment, standpoint, we live in a world of material abundance.

The final supposition on which we base our economic framework is an outgrowth of our first assumption, human worth, and of our knowledge that individual creativity underlies all forms of economic activity. It is the concept of *creative expression*.

As human beings, we are driven to grow and learn, to move forward, to evolve to states of greater autonomy and consciousness. For reasons grounded in the evolution of consciousness view, we are compelled to try new avenues of thought and action. We are driven to reinvent our world and ourselves. Human creativity is intrinsic to our nature. Our desire to create is fundamental to our essence, central to what makes us human.[7]

---

7. See *Book 1, Evolution of Consciousness*, chapter 11.

Moreover—given our physical embodiment, the nature of the creative process, and our existence in a physical universe—our desire to create must reveal itself in a tangible way. Consciousness in action manifests in time and space.[8] Our dreams and desires must result in an external, or physical, expression—in an economic activity. This expression will be as varied as the creativity that brought it into being. The building of a house is an expression of our creative drive. The nursing of a patient is an expression of our creative drive. The teaching of a child is an expression of our creative drive. The raising of a family is an expression of our creative drive. The writing of a novel or of a book on economics is an expression of our creative drive. Our economic expression is as diverse as we are unique, as varied as our dreams.

As such, our economic expression is as abundant as the creative activity that brought it into being. We are as prolific as we are creative. The greater our creative activity, the greater its impact on our material world. Our level of creative activity, in turn, shows a direct relationship to the freedom we provide for its action. The greater the freedom we enjoy as individuals, and thus the greater the opportunity we have to creatively express ourselves, the greater the amount and originality of the goods and services that results. Economic output is a function of human creativity, which is a function of the freedom and opportunity we provide the individual.

Our economics of fulfillment ideology is based on the assumption of economic expression. It is the notion that when we have the freedom and thus the opportunity to fulfill our creative needs we, as an unavoidable consequence, will fulfill our material needs. Justified by the evolution of consciousness view and the mechanism of the creative process, it is the belief that when we maximize our freedom to grow and learn and to express our creative nature, we, by virtue of our nature as evolving beings in an evolving universe, will maximize our material well-being.

There we have it, the three assumptions on which our economics of fulfillment philosophy rests: human worth, abundance, and economic expression. We are creative beings that exist in a physical construct brought into being by the trial and error and the creative building on and discarding of the old that is the creative process. The universe evolves through the evolution of humanity, and humanity evolves through the evolution

---

8. Ibid., chapters 2, 3, and 4.

of the individual. Wealth is the outcome of our creativity—as diverse as we are unique, as abundant as we are creative.

Our three assumptions reflect our understanding of the universe and of our place within the universe. They also embody all that is necessary to create an economic philosophy designed to accommodate the human community in all its diversity and exuberance. In socialism, human creativity is motivated by an individual's need to fit into society. In capitalism, human creativity is motivated by an individual's need for profit and wealth. In economics of fulfillment, human creativity is motivated by the most powerful of our desires—by the need we feel to follow our passion, by the yearning we feel to do that which we find meaningful and which brings fulfillment into our lives. From the above observations, we derive the guiding principle of the economics of fulfillment philosophy:

> The objective of the economics of fulfillment ideology is to create the social and economic conditions that provide the freedom and opportunity for every individual to evolve to his or her highest state of being and that by doing so allow humanity to evolve to its highest state of being.

In our economics of fulfillment philosophy, our ability to create and produce is an outcome of who we are as individuals, of our nature as human beings, of our drive to learn and to advance to greater awareness and substance of character. We have the ability to reshape our world in any way we desire and to produce material prosperity to the limits of our imagination and creative power. Human creativity—that which is at the heart of all economic activity—is the objective of our economic philosophy. Wealth as we have never before experienced it will be the outcome.

6

A Simple Economic Model

REASONABLY, WE COULD DEVISE many systems of economic practice that meet the objectives embodied in the guiding principle of the economics of fulfillment ideology. For the sake of example, in this chapter we will outline what may be the simplest, a model that in a direct way illustrates how we can give our economic philosophy tangible form. Though basic to the extreme, our model demonstrates what is most important, a way to provide the freedom we need to unleash our innate creative capacity and the physical expression that results.

To develop our economic system, we begin by expanding the home construction example that we touched on earlier. Imagine you are a homebuilder, hopefully one who builds houses out of bricks and reinforced concrete rather than out of two-by-sixes and wafer-board.

As a homebuilder, what is your motivation? Under a socialistic system, it would be to meet a state or corporate quota. Under a capitalistic system, it would be to make a profit. Under economics of fulfillment, your motivation would be intrinsic. Like the artist who is compelled to paint, you build homes because it is what you want to do in life. You enjoy ideals of form and shape and take pleasure in standards of architectural beauty. You are proud of what you create, and you build to your aesthetic and structural standards—higher standards, in your view, than any in the industry. To you, the home is a product of your artisanship. It is a creative work, an expression of your values and of your ingenuity and engineering skill. Building gives you satisfaction. It is the medium through which you evolve as a human being. You build because it is your passion.

Now, imagine that you and everyone else in your community maintain an account at the local "economics of fulfillment" bank, and that everyone's balance in their account is zero dollars. Next, you go to the owner of the builder's supply outlet and purchase 50 thousand dollars of bricks, concrete, steel rebar, and other materials.

So, who is the owner of the builder's supply outlet? Why is she in business? What is her motivation? The owner of the builder's supply does what she does because her passion in life is to run a business. She enjoys interacting with her customers and coworkers. These people share her interest in materials, engineering, and construction, and she thrives on assisting in their personal growth. She also thrives on learning about new materials and on interacting with manufacturers to develop products that work for her customers. Her creative expression is her business. She is an organizer, and she takes pride when things run smoothly.

As such, she manages her business in a different way than she would in a scarcity-based economic environment. She is not accountable to creditors, shareholders, bill collectors, and government regulators. She has no need to run her business to generate the greatest amount of income with the least amount of expense. Her motivation is to operate her business in a way that gives her the most personal satisfaction. She carries the best products and interacts with her coworkers and customers in a way that creates the most fulfilling relationships. As a manager, she is open to new ideas and to new ways of doing things. She is also not afraid to backtrack when something does not work. In our economics of fulfillment economy, there is no financial risk to her trial and error. Her business practices do not conflict with her social beliefs and her ethical standards.

Back at the bank, your account is reduced by 50 thousand dollars for the construction materials you purchased, and the account of the owner of the builder's supply outlet is increased by 50 thousand dollars for the construction materials she sold.

Note, you run a negative balance. You are 50 thousand dollars in the hole. But you are not at an ordinary bank. For the sake of illustration, imagine a bank where every member of the economy is free to run a negative balance in his or her account.

Clearly, such a bank is not in business to show a profit. It does not generate monthly, quarterly, semi-annual, and annual income statements. What, then, motivates the banker? Unlike the financial leaders of today, our banker does not run his bank to get rich off his stock option. There are no profits to share. He does what he does for the same reason you do what you do and everyone in our economics of fulfillment economy does what he or she does. His position at the bank fulfills his creative needs. Like the owner of our builder's supply, he derives satisfaction by helping others realize their creative potential. He provides the economic structure those in the economy need to immerse themselves in their creative activities and, by doing so, fulfills his creative needs. He operates his bank because it is his passion.

Next, imagine you meet the local schoolteacher. To her satisfaction in life comes from bringing out the best in her pupils. She loves young people and thrives on their energy and freedom of thought. Her job is to create an environment where her students can express their creative drive. She wants them to learn what they find interesting and meaningful. To do this, our teacher experiments with new ways of interacting with her students and with new ways of structuring their learning experience. Like the owner of our builder's supply outlet, she is not afraid to try things and to backtrack when something does not work. How can she teach her students to maximize their creative potential unless she is free to maximize her creative potential? It is also important to our teacher that her students learn the skills they need to develop and express their creativity. She works hard on the basics: reading, writing, and mathematics. She also instills in her students the need to question and to reflect on what they hear and are taught. She knows that they must come to their own understanding of the world.

Our teacher fulfills her creative needs through the growth of her students, but she could not set a brick or mix a batch of mortar if her life depended on it and could care less about designing and building a house. So, you agree to sell her the home you are building for 100 thousand dollars. But how did you come up with this price? It was not based on the market. You had no need to see what other homes in the neighborhood were selling for. There are no forces of supply and demand to bid your price up or down. You had no cost of capital. Or, more precisely, no one charged you for the opportunity to build a house and to contribute to the economy. You based your price on the 50 thousand dollars you paid for the materials and 50 thousand dollars you felt would cover the cost of land and allow you a comfortable standard of living for your labor. We will call this price the *Fair Production Value.*

Your account at the bank is increased by 100 thousand dollars, giving you a balance of 50 thousand dollars. The teacher's account is reduced by 100 thousand dollars, giving her a negative balance of 100 thousand dollars. The owner of the builder's supply outlet has a balance of 50 thousand dollars. *Figure 7* summarizes the transactions that have taken place at our bank

Bank Account Balances

	Builder		Supplier		Teacher	
	(+)	(-)	(+)	(-)	(+)	(-)
Buy Materials		50	50			
Sell Home	100					100
	50		50			100

Fig. 7. Transactions. The above account balances illustrate the transactions at our economics of fulfillment bank. Note, the addition and subtraction transactions balance out. In an economics of fulfillment model, wealth per say is not the goal of economic activity. The objective of the economy is individual freedom and the opportunity to create wealth that individual freedom makes possible.

So, blueprints and materials in hand, you begin construction. This is an important time in your life. You have worked hard planning your house, and you are glad to start building. You enjoy laying the bricks, tying the reinforcement, and pouring the concrete. Day-by-day, your home takes shape: the foundation, the first floor, the second floor, the roof. You lay the floor tiles. You design and build the cabinetry. And, after the house is completed, you invite the banker, the teacher, and the owner of the builder's supply outlet over and share the satisfaction your project gave you with those that helped. The home you built for the teacher is an outcome of your creativity, but it is also the result of their creativity. It is a product of the economy.

The above example lays out a simple economics of fulfillment system. In our economy, there is a bank and a banker, a teacher, the owner of the builder's supply outlet, and you, the builder. We could include other elements. The banker and everyone else in the economy need groceries. This could involve a butcher, a fish market, and a produce stand. These could involve a farmer, a rancher, and a fisherman. The owner of the builder's supply outlet needs a truck to deliver her products, and someone must build and maintain the truck and provide it with oil and gasoline. In the real world, our economics of fulfillment economy would be vastly more complex. But the elements we included are sufficient to take a closer look at how our economy works.

The most striking aspect of our economics of fulfillment system is the ability to run a negative bank account balance. The idea of such runs contrary to everything we have been taught about economics and have experienced in life. But the value we place on money and the methods we use to account for money are not absolute. They are not set in nature. We invented and choose to follow them. To understand the idea of a negative bank account balance, we must come to terms with certain basic ideas associated with the concept:

First, as we mentioned, our bank is not in business to show a profit. Today's banks make money off of money. They borrow at a low interest rate and lend at a high interest rate. The banker's motivation is to increase his or her control over capital. In our model, the banker is not driven to maximize the power and wealth of his organization. His goal is to facilitate economic activity. Risk and return have no meaning. His ambition is to maximize the bank's role in the economy, not to make money. His purpose for being is to create opportunity.

Second, the ability to run a negative bank account balance is not welfare or a giveaway. It has nothing to do with taxes and socialistic wealth redistribution. In a socialist-capitalist economy, a welfare or other entitlement program uses the tax system backed by the police power of the state to take money from one group of people and give it to another. One can argue that this is necessary, but it does not change what it is, a redistribution of ownership. In our economics of fulfillment model, such shuffling of wealth has no meaning. We are not taking a little here and giving a little there. Everyone can run a negative bank account balance.

Third, the ability to run a negative bank account balance does not constitute a liability. In capitalism, those who perform the work purchase the right to contribute to the material well-being of the human community from those who control the capital. The cost to get our hands dirty is a share of the material wealth we create through our work. When a bank issues a loan, it does not give opportunity it sells opportunity. When you mortgage a house, you are not only paying for the house but for the privilege of paying for the house. When in our bank we run a negative bank account balance, we are not taking out a loan and incurring a liability. We do not have to apply for credit and write a business plan with the customary pie charts, bar graphs, and estimates of market demand and of future earnings and expenses. No one will weigh the risk of the bank's investment against our ability to pay it back. No one will question our credit history. No one will track our credit history. No one will turn us away, and no one will harass us if we miss a payment because there is no such thing as a payment.

Fourth, in an economy not based on scarcity, the concept of money does not mean what we typically take it to mean. In capitalism, money represents a claim to wealth—a hold on scarce resources. In our economics of fulfillment model, money has no value beyond its use as a tool to facilitate economic transaction. In our example, we added 50 thousand dollars of wealth to the economy because of our builder's labor. But, as the totals on *Figure 7* show, the cumulative figure in everyone's bank account balances out. It remains at zero. Even in today's scarcity-based economic world, someone must print money. Someone in effect must enter a negative balance in some account somewhere. Rather than to do so from the top down, by some government or other body keying-in a figure or manipulating the multiplier effect and schemes of debt purchase of monetary policy, our economy prints money at a lower economic level. We print money at the point of the transaction—when and in the amount needed.

The ability to run a negative bank account balance has nothing to do with profit, socialistic wealth redistribution, liability, or a scarcity-based interpretation of money. What, then, is it all about? In traditional economic terms, our ability to run a negative bank account balance breaks down the capital barrier. It integrates a mechanism of capital redistribution, and thus opportunity creation, into the economy at the point of the transaction. In capitalism, those who control the capital decide where they will invest and thus exercise control over the economy. They decide who will contribute to the economy and for what reason. The mechanism of a negative bank account balance takes this power out of the hands of the capitalized and places it in the hands of the individual. It transfers power from the elite to every member of the economy. It provides the freedom we need to maximize our creative expression, ending the need for loans, stock exchanges, and other sources of investment funds.

The concept of a negative bank account balance challenges our most deeply ingrained notions of what an economy is and how it works. As simple yet as difficult as it is to get a handle on, the technique illustrates the fundamental philosophical difference between a scarcity-based model and an economics of fulfillment model. In socialism-capitalism, wealth is the object of value, not the act of producing wealth. In economics of fulfillment, wealth is the byproduct of economic activity, the outcome of what we cherish the most—our freedom and individuality and the creative expression our freedom and individuality allow us to bring forth.

This carries our discussion to certain related points about our economics of fulfillment model, ideas that will further contrast our economic system with a scarcity-based economic system and illustrate the nature of money and economic function.

If making money is not the objective of our economy, why do we have a bank and assign a value to our transactions? What meaning does fair production value or for that matter any price have in an economic system where anyone can run a negative balance in his or her bank account? From a strictly economics of fulfillment standpoint, our bank has no purpose and our monetary valuation of transactions has no meaning, but we include them for a reason. Monetary valuation allows our system to import and export to an existing scarcity-based economy. Our model transforms money into the tool that, as in the chapters ahead we will describe, we use to transition from a socialist-capitalist world into an economics of fulfillment world.

Like a socialist or capitalist economic model, our economics of fulfillment economy is a set of rules. It is an agreed upon way of conducting our economic lives. In our simple model, we must maintain a bank account, and the bank must record transactions and allow a negative account balance. In contrast to a scarcity-based system, however, the degree of regulation is minimal. Our economy has a simpler set of rules. Businesses do not battle for profit, and government does not struggle to balance competing interests, create a level playing field for business, and in the larger sense keep the economy from unraveling. Because there is nothing for factions to compete for, there is no need for the vast body of laws and regulations that we face in a scarcity-based system.

Our economy also aligns business and social interests. Our builder has no incentive to build a poorly constructed house or to use environmentally damaging materials. He also has no incentive to build a house that is affordable to only the rich. In our builder's mind, his home is not a product targeted to the most profitable market. It is an artistic and engineering achievement. As such, how can he build any but the best? Architecture is dictated by tastes and by the neighborhood and the size and configuration of the building site and not by the market. Engineering is determined by the home's environment. Our builder is free to construct his house to withstand the stresses imposed by the ecosystem in which he is building and by doing so integrates his home into the environment.[1] Some people prefer large houses; others prefer small houses. Free from the demands of capitalistic profit and socialistic conformity, builders create the type of homes they find satisfying to construct and sell. They build big houses and little houses, but there is no such thing as an upscale unit and an entry-level unit.

This brings us to the essence of our economics of fulfillment system. The heart of our economy is freedom. In our economy, members enjoy an unprecedented level of control over their lives. The schoolteacher does what she does not to make a living but because she loves to teach. The builder does what he does not to support his family but because he loves to build. The banker and the owner of the builder's supply outlet do what they do because their activities fulfill their creative needs. No one in our economy is labor and no one is management. There may be task divisions. Our builder can hire a bricklayer. But our bricklayer is not labor. He does not work to make us money. Like our builder, his passion is construction. His craft is bricklaying, but at least at the moment he has no desire to engineer and build an entire house. In our economy, no one is a component of the economy. No one is a cog in the production process of land, labor, and capital. Everyone contributes to the economy, and the economy allows everyone to fulfill their creative and thus material needs. To emphasize a point worth restating: in socialism, the individual has no motivation to contribute to the economy other than political conformity. In capitalism, the individual is motivated by the artificial construct of money and profit. Our economics of fulfillment model provides the freedom for the individual to be motivated in the most deeply felt way, by his or her calling in existence.

We began the chapter by reflecting on the guiding principle of the economics of fulfillment philosophy. We then devised a simple economic system that adhered to the ideals embodied in this principle. In our economy, there was a bank and a banker, a builder, a schoolteacher, and the

---

1. See *Book 3, Blueprint for Reconstruction*, chapter 6.

owner of the builder's supply. The accounting mechanism of running a negative bank account balance provided the framework for our economic activity. It gave every member of the economy the means to evolve to his or her potential and by doing so gave the human community the means to evolve to its potential. This brings us to the obvious question. How, in the "real world," could such a free and self-directed economy ever work?

7

Feasibility of a New Economics

IN THE LAST CHAPTER, we developed a simple economic system designed to meet the objectives embodied in the guiding principle of our emerging economics of fulfillment ideology. No doubt, many readers found our system esoteric, idealistic, impractical. Our simple economic model may have been intriguing. It may have even sounded reasonable on paper, but how could such a free and self-regulated approach to economic activity work in the real world? In this chapter, we reflect on the feasibility of our economic system and philosophy.

Our discussion begins with two questions that by now most of us have asked and that sum up the difficulty people have understanding how our economic model will work. First, what in our economics of fulfillment system would keep one person from buying up everything and running a huge negative balance at the bank? Second, what, in our system, would keep someone from sitting in front of the television and not contributing to the economy?

A philosophy, economic or otherwise, expresses an understanding of the universe or of some aspect of the universe. It is a set of concepts that tells us about the world. We derived our economics of fulfillment philosophy from the larger evolution of consciousness vision and encapsulated our insight in the economics of fulfillment principle. In contrast, an economic system is an agreed upon way of conducting economic activity based on a deeper philosophical understanding of the world. An economic system structures our economic lives through a body of laws, standards, and regulations based on an underlying philosophy.

In today's global economy, economic systems function under a Darwinian, scarcity-based understanding of the world, expressed through our use of and the value we place on money. We assign almost every transaction a monetary value. Money is the lifeblood of existence. When the flow of money in our lives is interrupted, the consequences are devastating. In today's world, money—and the power it represents—is in many respects the overriding human motivation. We see this in divisions of wealth and control, in excesses of consumption, and in political decisions that place economic interests over human interests. Money defines our place in the human community. Money is how we determine who is fit to be a member of the human community. Justified by our worldview and the economic practices it supports, today's global economy is driven by money.

But the world of today is not the world that will exist hours, days, weeks, months, and years from now. Central to the transformation of our world is the "threshold to meaning." We have talked about this point of transformation before, but not in the most down-to-earth terms. From a practical standpoint, our transcendence to meaning begins when we realize that our way of life is not set in stone. It starts when we accept or at least open ourselves to the possibility that we can move beyond old ideas and old ways of doing things and create a better world. At the moment we embrace meaning—or at least at the moment when we become aware of it and direct our lives and creative energy toward its realization—we undergo a transformation. We no longer frame our existence in the materialistic terms school and society have driven into our consciousness.

This brings us back to our original two questions. If we were to implement our economics of fulfillment system for the people of today, nothing would prevent one person from buying up everything and running a huge negative balance in their bank account. Similarly, nothing would prevent us from devoting our lives to the soap operas. Our economic system could not function if its members saw themselves as locked in a competition for material wealth or if its members placed a value on doing nothing and taking advantage of the system. Some would fight to be the one who came out on top. Others would be content to live off the work of their fellows.

Accumulation of wealth, consumption for the sake of consumption, and retirement for the sake of retirement, however, are not values we are born with. They are values we are taught. They are not intrinsic to our nature as creative beings but are ingrained in our psyche by the dynamics of scarcity-based economics. We are autonomous beings, but we are not by nature lazy or greedy beings.

In one sense, our idea of a negative bank account balance is nothing more than an accounting gimmick. Any technique we substitute, however, must perform a similar capital redistribution and money printing func-tion. In whatever form we implement our economics of fulfillment system, however, it cannot work unless the members of our economy look beyond a materialistic vision of the universe, beyond traditional ideas of money and economic function. Meaning in the esoteric sense of transcendence to a state of evolutionary consciousness is not a prerequisite. Meaning will catalyze economics of fulfillment, and economics of fulfillment will catalyze meaning.

But the members of the economy must embrace the assumptions on which our economic philosophy is based. We must abandon the idea of resource scarcity and accept the idea of material abundance. We must embrace our creative nature, believe our creativity will manifest in some form of economic expression, and accept the value of the human being. Economics of fulfillment provides unprecedented control over our lives. For an economics of fulfillment system to work, the individual must ac-cept the responsibility for this control. We must believe in ourselves. We must believe in the importance of our role in creating a better future for ourselves, for our families, and for the human community. How farfetched is it to think that given the opportunity we would structure our lives and direct our creative energy to fulfilling our passion? By our evolution to greater consciousness and substance of character, economics of fulfill-ment becomes a feasible ideology. Our economics of fulfillment system is not for the people of today. It is for the people we are today becoming.

To gain a deeper understanding of the above conclusion, it would be useful to explore and contrast two elements of economic behavior com-mon to scarcity-based and economics of fulfillment ideologies—*competi-tion* and *cooperation.*

We begin with an obvious distinction. Economic competition is not the same as athletic competition. There are similarities, but on the surface. It is hard to find much to criticize about the neighborhood soccer game or the high school track meet, though many will argue this point and we often use athletic competition to instill deeper competitive values. But athletic competition is not economic competition. In athletic competi-tion, the rules are clear. There will be winners and losers, but based on a score. Athletic competition is a game. You may lose today; but, if you practice and work hard, next week or season it will be your turn to stand on the victory podium. When not corrupted by money and turned into an economic battleground, athletic competition is a medium through which we strive for personal betterment and, with respect to a team sport, achieve such through cooperation with others.

In today's scarcity-based, socialist-capitalist economic framework, competition and cooperation are altogether different. Competition is the value we embrace as a society that it is acceptable to have winners and losers. It is the notion that it is okay to leave some behind, that not all members of the human community are entitled to wealth, success, opportunity, and a decent life. In economic competition, the consequences of losing are a matter of our continued existence. Death allows no rematch. Economic competition is the imposition of Darwin's mechanism of natural selection onto our social order. Economic competition is our version of survival of the fittest. It is our willingness to accept casualties in a battle against one another we wage out of ignorance and out of fear to create a better way.

So ingrained is our notion of economic competition and so profound is its impact on our lives that it shapes our understanding of cooperation. In a scarcity-based economy, cooperation takes place in two ways: It is imposed through government or through some regulatory body to fulfill what one or another political faction deems a social need. A government entitlement program compels citizens to fund a retirement system, healthcare plan, or other social program. Cooperation also takes place when members of the economy align to compete against other members. A company or corporation is a group of people who merge their talents to compete with another group with similar objectives and if possible to put them out of business and create a monopoly. In today's economic environment, cooperation is a dimension of competition.

Competition and cooperation also exist in our economics of fulfillment model, but they mean something different. In our economy, economic competition is like athletic competition in the most positive sense. It is our path to growth and perfection. An athlete strives for a faster time or a higher score. Our teacher strives to interact with her students in a better way. The owner of our builder's supply strives to make her business run more smoothly. Our builder strives to make each house better than his last. In an economics of fulfillment world, we compete with ourselves to better ourselves. Competition is our drive to grow, learn, and evolve.

In our economics of fulfillment economy, we also compete with one another, but not for profit, market share, or other contrived measure of success. We do not compete to surpass the creativity of another but, as would a member of an athletic team, to bring out the best in those around us and achieve a higher end. Our builder competes to advance the art of house construction. He strives to improve his personal standards and by doing so to improve the standards of the building industry. This relationship between individual betterment and human betterment has a remarkable outcome. Unlike in a scarcity-based world, competition does not force cooperation. Competition manifests in cooperation. Our builder can only realize the full benefits of a new building technique if he shares his knowledge with his peers, and the technique makes its way into the construction industry. Betterment demands openness.

In our economics of fulfillment system, no one is left behind. There are no winners and losers. Should not this be what an economy is about? Should not an economy be an exchange of resources and abilities to meet human material and higher needs? Over the course of evolution, human social structure has become less collective. Cooperation is an outcome of evolution. Greater individuality—a greater sense of self and purpose and not socialistic ideals of uniformity and central control—create a more cooperative society.

Centuries ago, the economist Adam Smith put forth the principle of the "invisible hand." In it, he stated that the individual's actions in the pursuit of self-interest would, as if guided by an invisible hand, be in the interest of the economy. This principle has no meaning in an economics of fulfillment system where self-interest is not measured by profit and wealth, but we can put forth a related idea. The individual, in the pursuit of his or her creative interests, will generate the conditions that allow every individual to pursue their creative interests. Economics of fulfillment provides the opportunity for us to fulfill our most deeply felt needs—desires that in a scarcity-based economy we may spend a lifetime attempting to satisfy through materialism and the accumulation of wealth but can never succeed. Competition and cooperation are aspects of our calling to follow our passion in life and by doing so to better the world around us.

The last point we need to discuss concerning the feasibility of our economic system is the idea of *efficiency*. In our economics of fulfillment model, no mechanism exists to weigh the costs and benefits of an economic activity. There is no incentive to compare capital investment against market value and capital return. How, then, in our economy do we operate efficiently?

To answer this question, we begin with a look at efficiency in traditional economic terms. In a scarcity-based economic system, economists define efficiency as the ability to get the most out of an economic activity by putting in the least, measured in dollars. A business that employs the minimum number of workers needed to manufacture a product is said to run more efficiently than one that refuses to layoff workers. The additional labor cost leads to a higher cost per unit of production. This decreases the company's profit and threatens its competitive position. The same idea of efficiency applies to the economy as a whole. During the 1990s, politicians held up the United States economy as a model for the world. In that decade, the productivity of the American worker soared. The worker spent more hours on the job and produced greater economic output for proportionately lower wages. In this respect, the above definition of efficiency relates to what economists call *full-employment*. An economy where every member is employed is said to maximize per capita output. Politicians and economists pay a lot of attention to unemployment figures. To a large extent, fiscal and monetary policy are devoted to keeping these figures at a reasonable level and thus to minimizing their political fallout.

The difficulty with the dollars-in and dollars-out measure of economic efficiency is that it fails to account for every aspect of economic activity. In particular, it does not embrace the value of the human being and the variable of human motivation. A worker at a firm may be motivated to perform out of fear of job loss and the threat to survival job loss represents, but this motivation is external. It is not intrinsic to the task at hand. The worker shows up to work to keep from being fired but may feel no passion for the job and consequently put no more than minimal effort into it. Similarly, measures of unemployment do not take into account a related form of inefficiency. When a person has a job, his or her name does not show up on the unemployment roster. You are employed or not. Though attempts have been made to account for this, unemployment figures typically do not consider the relationship between the job and the employee's abilities. As it is often said, how many people with advanced degrees make their living mopping floors or flipping burgers?

An efficient economy is not one that generates the greatest capital output with the least capital input. It is not an economy that has a contrived measure of zero unemployment. An efficient economy exists when every member of the economy devotes his or her energies to the fullest extent of his or her abilities. This is achieved through freedom. In an efficient economy, every member has the opportunity to develop their interests and to align their creative energy with their economic activities. This is true productivity. This is what efficiency fundamentally means. Maximum economic efficiency can only be obtained when every member of the economy has the freedom and thus the opportunity to follow his or her calling in life.

A scarcity-based economy, therefore, could never operate in a truly efficient manner. When we are consumers and components of the production process, we are locked in an economic position. The average individual is too busy earning a living to follow his or her passion. By nature, a scarcity-based economic system is an inefficient system. Politicians and economists ignore this aspect of contemporary economic function. They invent measures of economic performance that circumvent efficiency's true nature.

As free as our economics of fulfillment ideology may be, however, our actions are not entirely unrestrained. Our builder faces limits, but they are not imposed from the outside. They are self-imposed, a product of engineering, architecture and of our builder's knowledge of economic function. No government regulation may prevent our builder from constructing his home with twelve-foot thick walls, but that is a lot of concrete to mix and poor. From an engineering and architectural standpoint, it makes no sense to consume these resources, as abundant as sand, gravel, clay, and limestone may be. Neither would it be responsible for the builder to do so from the standpoint of the economy. In the time it takes to build one house with twelve-foot thick walls, he could build several houses with two-foot thick walls, and both designs would survive the worst earthquake or the fiercest tornado or hurricane. Multiply houses would also allow the builder to refine his craft and to further satisfy his creative needs.

The notion of efficiency reveals something about an economics of fulfillment system that economists as far back as Adam Smith have thought about but that in a scarcity-based world has proven unobtainable. In our economy, every member has the opportunity to direct their creative energy toward their passion and accepts the responsibility to do so in a reasonable way. As a result, every member is employed to the fullest extent of his or her abilities, and we produce material wealth to the limits of our creative potential. By its nature, an economics of fulfillment system does what socialism and capitalism cannot, self-regulate to optimal efficiency. When we maximize freedom and opportunity, we maximize economic output.

In socialism and capitalism, a ruling group empowered by law and capital control our economic behavior. In our economics of fulfillment model, we, the individual, control our economic behavior. Economic interaction reflects our level of evolutionary development and social organization. The justification for our philosophy lies in the evolution of consciousness view. It rests on our acceptance of who we are: on the value we assign to ourselves as human beings and on the individual responsibility for our actions this value embodies.

In this section of the book, we introduced an economic philosophy that is not based on supply, demand, and central control. Perhaps the most useful aspect of our discussion was that it allowed us to reflect on economics outside the box of contemporary thought—the opportunity to grapple with the idea that our world may not be as we have been taught and that there may be other ways to go about our lives. This carries us to our next objective. We have described how a simple economic system based on our economic philosophy might work. Our task now becomes to look at how we will implement a free and open economy in a socialist-capitalist world.

PART THREE

Implementation

8

Early Systems

W E HAVE LAID OUT the economics of fulfillment philosophy and introduced a system of economic activity designed to function under that philosophy. In this section of the book, we look at how we will implement our economic ideology. What will the first economics of fulfillment systems be like and through what steps will we put them into place? What educational and governmental structures must we establish to support their function and expansion? When we come to the understanding that our world is one of material abundance and that every human being is essential to the evolution of the human community, we are struck by a realization. Economics of fulfillment is more than an economic ideology. It has a deeper significance with respect to the evolutionary transcendence taking place within us—a role in humankind's social and personal evolution that is pivotal to our future.

Before we delve into this conclusion and the nuts-and-bolts of starting the world's first economics of fulfillment economy, it would be worthwhile to talk about how we will not start such a system. The future awaits our invention and we cannot be sure of our path to the future, but it is reasonable to deem certain methods of implementation less practical. In this way, we narrow our task to the most reasonable way to start a new economy.

Above all, we can rule out government as initiating the first economics of fulfillment systems. In the United States, the passing of a bill to allow for such commonsense things as tax reform, energy production, or healthy forest management can be tied up by special interests for decades and when legislation is passed do nothing more than pander to those interests. It is difficult to envision the leadership of any nation overcoming the cultural and political barriers necessary to reinvent a nation's economy. If such leadership were to emerge, it would probably not take place in a developed nation where the political establishment is entrenched but in a country faced with economic breakdown. As we read and hear about every day, there are a growing number of nations in this position. The tendency on the part of leadership in these nations, however, has been to stabilize economic conditions by aligning with corporate interests and more secure economies. A move on the part of a nation to take economic matters into its own hands and to put the interests of the nation and population before those of multinational business and environmental and other global concerns would be exceedingly bold.

Another way the first economics of fulfillment systems will probably not emerge is through armed revolt. A century-and-a-half ago, Marx wrote that socialism would emerge from capitalism after a revolution of the proletariat. Those with the means of production would not share their wealth and power without a fight. In certain respects, history has proven Marx correct. To this day, those with capital go to whatever lengths are necessary to maintain their control over capital. Capitalism may be a transitional system. Economics of fulfillment, however, is not socialism. Our economic philosophy embodies a shift in thought so fundamental that it goes beyond a socialist-capitalist scramble for wealth and control. Economics of fulfillment rests on a new vision of the universe. Like any truth, this vision cannot be imposed. An individual must embrace the economics of fulfillment doctrine in his or her own way. An imposition of economic ideology through armed revolt—unless rooted in an evolutionary uplifting of the population and not the outcome of revolutionaries invoking a cause—does not accomplish this goal.

If the first economics of fulfillment systems will not begin through government policy or through some form of violent revolutionary uprising, how will they start? Because of the personal nature of the economics of fulfillment philosophy, and the degree of personal responsibility the function of an economics of fulfillment system will require, the first systems will almost certainly emerge on a local level, from the bottom up.

In many parts of the world, including the developed nations, it has become increasingly difficult to make a living under socialism and capitalism. In the United States, once high paying technology and manufacturing jobs have gone oversees or are performed by low-wage immigrant labor. By almost any measure, the standard of living for significant sectors of the middle class in that nation has declined since the early 1970s. As uncertainty grows and trade, entitlement, and capital redistribution systems further break down, it will become even harder to earn a living.

Similarly, as we cross the threshold to meaning, our expectations concerning work will change. To a greater extent than today, we will be unwilling to accept unfulfilling assembly line and other jobs for no other reason than to earn a paycheck. Moreover, as technical and other skilled jobs scatter throughout the globe, the economy in the United States and other developed nations has produced a growing number of menial service jobs. Even today, many young people choose to stay in school, often massing tremendous debt, because the economy provides no satisfying alternative. As we come to see ourselves in less materialistic terms, we will expect more out of our careers than our parents expected and that the scarcity-based economy is able to deliver.

Faced with growing economic uncertainty and changing expectations, we will be compelled to question the status quo and to seek new ways to do things. As this process matures and people realize that they must look beyond existing economic and governmental structures and traditional ways of doing things to create a better life, they will join to form economic groups based on the economics of fulfillment model—groups that they structure to meet their creative and material needs. These local economics of fulfillment systems will not replace existing socialist and capitalist systems but, at least initially, exist within and import and export to these systems. We will implement the first economics of fulfillment systems close to home, among ourselves.

How, then, will this reinvention of economics take place? We are a founding member of the first economics of fulfillment system. Where do we begin?

As the economic model we developed in the last section illustrates, our economy has a structure. Based on this, step one of economic implementation becomes clear. We *create a bank*. Without a bank to track our economic activity, we have no framework. There is no structure on which to hang our transactions.

But creating a bank is not an easy thing to do. If we could isolate our economy from the global socialist-capitalist economy, it would be a simple matter to open a bank. Our bank could be as basic as an accounting program run on a computer. Its implementation would involve little more than writing the program, creating a chart of accounts, and devising ways to update account balances. To create a bank in the scarcity-based environment in which our economy must exist and interact, however, is an involved task. We begin by researching how to create a bank. What are the laws and requirements in our political jurisdiction? How will our bank transfer funds: cash, checks, debit and credit cards or their equivalent, electronically?

After we have determined the legal procedures to create a bank in our part of the world, we can go ahead and form our bank. We can write an accounting program and open an account for each member of our economy. But the member accounts will need to be more complex than those in last section's example. For our economy to interact with the socialist-capitalist framework in which we have implemented it, we must isolate internal economics of fulfillment activities, the transactions that take place between members of the economy, from external economics of fulfillment activities, the transactions that take place between members and the scarcity-based world. Thus, as *Figure 8* shows, our bank statement would have to include two balances, one for economics of fulfillment dollars and one for scarcity-based dollars. Correspondingly, our bank would have to track and calculate two sets of cumulative balances.

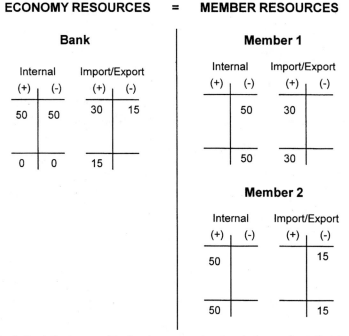

Fig. 8. Bank Statement. The bank must maintain a balance sheet that tracks internal economic transactions and import and export transactions.

With our bank in place, we can move on and implement step two of economic implementation. Next, we must *establish a cash fund*. It is one thing to create a bank and to put into place the framework of our economy. It is another to use that framework. This requires capital. Money has little meaning within our economy. It simply facilitates a transaction. But to create an economics of fulfillment economy in a scarcity-based environment, we must have enough cash on hand to interact with that environment. The exact amount of the economy's startup fund is difficult to say and would vary between nations and jurisdictions, but it must be sufficient to support the economy until it generates enough activity to exist on its own and to import and export in a manageable way.

With our bank in place and sufficient outside currency available, we have established the groundwork for step three of economic implementation: We begin *economic activity*.

To see how this works, we need to learn more about the men and women with whom we founded our economy. Certain members of our economy will devote their energy to managing the economy. They will fill the role of the banker in our earlier example. Others will have different interests, which is one of the reasons we started our economy. The scarcity-based system in which we worked did not provide the resources and opportunity to direct our lives as we saw fit. We also know that food, housing, clothing, and healthcare are among our essential needs and for this reason will play a role in our economy. Let us say that, in addition to those who work in our bank and who are responsible for the accounting structure of our economy, our colleagues include a nurse, a farmer, a builder, and a clothing designer, each of whom wants to start a business.

This is where our pool of outside currency comes into play. To open a medical practice, our nurse needs to buy medical supplies and equipment. To grow food, our farmer needs to buy a tractor, fertilizer, and pesticides. To build homes, our builder needs to buy land and materials. To make clothes, our clothing designer needs to buy cloth, thread, buttons, zippers, and a sewing machine. In a way, starting our economy is like starting a business in a scarcity-based system. Because we must draw resources from the outside socialist-capitalist economy, we must have startup capital. But if we properly manage our economy, we will grow beyond the need for scarcity-based resources and free ourselves from the limitations imposed by the outside world.

So, the nurse provides healthcare to the farmer, builder, clothing designer, and those who run the bank. The farmer provides food. The builder provides shelter. The bankers maintain our economic structure, and the clothing designer makes sure we all have something nice to wear. Every member of our economy conducts transactions as they see fit, and every member is free to run a negative balance in their bank account. By pursuing their own creative interests, the members of the economy fulfill their creative needs and provide for everyone's material needs. We have accomplished our goal. Our economy is a functioning economics of fulfillment system, but our work is not yet done. Our economy is not a sustainable economics of fulfillment system.

This brings us to step four of economic implementation: *regulation*. So long as economic activity is limited to transactions between members, and so long as the assumptions on which our economics of fulfillment ideology are based prove to be correct, our economy can run without oversight. It would self-regulate to optimal efficiency in accordance with the dynamics of an economics of fulfillment system. But, because our economy is yet too small to meet all of our material needs, we must regulate imports and exports to maintain a reserve of outside currency. For our economy to grow and prosper, the value in our bank's scarcity-based cumulative account must be positive and sufficient to meet the economy's obligations to the scarcity-based world.

We can accomplish this in two ways. First, we can reduce the amount of goods we import and thus decrease our need for outside currency; and, second, we can increase the amount of goods we export and thus bring outside currency into our economy.

To reduce imports, we need to incorporate the means of production into our economy. Rather than buy drugs and medical supplies from a corporation, we can invite chemists and researchers to join our economy and create our own medical supply industry. Similarly, our builder needs sand and gravel and buys them from a quarry where they are dug and crushed. The rock crushing business is competitive. The owner likes his work but not the environment in which he must operate. We open an account for him at the bank, and he becomes a member of our economy. He enjoys the freedom to run his business to the highest standards and in the most personally satisfying manner, and he and everyone in our economy benefit from decreased reliance on scarcity-based resources.

To increase exports, on the other hand, we must be free to sell to the outside economy. Our clothing manufacturer may sell pants, shirts, and dresses to people outside the economy. Our builder may sell houses to people outside the economy. Our nurse may see patients that are not members of our economics of fulfillment community. Similarly, there is no reason why a person in our economy cannot work outside the economy. Our nurse may wish to enjoy the lifestyle our economy provides but rather than start her own practice and, at least at this point in her life, take on the demands of running a business may prefer to work at an outside hospital. She reaps the benefits of being a member of an economics of fulfillment community; and, with the deposit of her paycheck in our bank, the economy reaps the benefit of scarcity-based currency. A related situation exists for a person or a couple on a retirement income. He, she, or they may enjoy the benefits of our economy, which will almost certainly be greater than they could otherwise afford, and continue to draw their pension. In both examples, our economy meets the needs of its members, and the members bring in outside capital.

During our economy's formative period, economic management will be a balancing act between inflows and outflows of scarcity-based currency with the objective to manage cash reserves to maintain economic stability and to make available the outside resources necessary for economic expansion.

This brings us to the fifth step in implementing our economics of fulfillment system. For us to manage our economy and assure its growth, we must know what is going on within our economy. At some point in the implementation of our economics of fulfillment system, possibly at the time we created our bank, we must put into place an *information system*.

The nature of our information system and the way we use it, however, is fundamentally different from such a system and the way we would employ it in a socialist-capitalist economy or institution. To manage imports and exports, we may be inclined to think that those in charge of the economy, presumably our bankers, must gather data and based on this information decide who should buy from the outside economy and who should sell to the outside economy. This approach, however, conflicts with the values embodied in the economics of fulfillment doctrine. In our economy, economic regulation is not imposed from the top down. There is no all-powerful leadership, no ruling elite. Our bankers do not control economic activity; they fulfill their creative needs by facilitating economic activity. Our information system does not monitor and regulate. It provides the individual with the knowledge he or she needs to conduct his or her economic affairs to assure economic growth and stability.

Our builder, for example, may decide to sell every second or third home he constructs to the outside economy to offset his rebar purchases. Our farmer may decide to sell a percentage of his crop to the outside economy to offset his fertilizer purchases. Our sand and gravel crusher may decide to sell a portion of his product to the outside economy to cover his property taxes. In a scarcity-based system, everyone is in competition with everyone else. Some form of central control, or overall regulatory structure, is necessary. In our economy, no one is at odds. Our success does not depend on someone else's failure. As diverse as our creative and material needs may be, we can orchestrate their fulfillment to address the interests of the larger economy. If our economy falls victim to its scarcity-based environment, we lose the freedom we enjoy and that our economy provides. The success of our economy is a function of open management and of individual responsibility. Every member takes on the responsibility for economic management. With freedom, it is in our economic self-interest to conduct our affairs for the good of all.

How, then, do we structure an information system to meet our needs? To some extent, we have already put into place a system that can do this. In its simplest form, our information system would provide the member with his or her account balances and with the cumulative balances that summarize overall economic activity. We could of course supplement this information. Import and export trends would help us determine how much of our creative efforts we should channel outside the economy. Data for other businesses in our industry would also be useful, as would the goals and decisions of others in the economy. In a broader sense, a vibrant and critical press is necessary, staffed by members of the journalism profession who fulfill their creative needs by delving into, reporting on, and above all critically examining our economic activities. We need analysis. We need opinion. We need to look at the workings of our economy from every possible angle. Our information system must be diverse and flexible. It must be run as an aspect of the economy, and it must be designed for the benefit of the individual member. Our information system must provide us with the data we need to responsibly manage our affairs as our economy grows and evolves.

In this respect, our information system serves a higher purpose than data accumulation and presentation. Unlike in a scarcity-based system, we are not subservient to the economy. No one needs to keep-tabs on our behavior or to place limits on our economic activity. By providing every member with the knowledge to align his or her economic activities with the interests of the economy, our information system creates within the member an awareness of the economy. In evolution of consciousness terms, it invokes within us a sense of where the economy is at and of how we can contribute to its function. Our information system sustains the body of our economy.

This completes our look at the steps required to implement the first economics of fulfillment systems. Such systems will probably not emerge through government or armed revolt but on a local level, from the bottom up. To form the first economics of fulfillment systems and to integrate them into the scarcity-based global economy we must perform five tasks: We create a bank and by doing so erect the framework of our economy. We establish a startup fund sufficient to allow our economy to interact during its formative period with its scarcity-based environment. With these measures in place, we have established the economic structure we need to open businesses and to conduct transactions. To assure the stability of our economic system, we must regulate imports and exports to maintain a reserve of outside funds sufficient for economic function and expansion. This requires an information system that provides the individual member with the knowledge needed to manage his or her economic affairs. The steps we outlined are broad. Their implementation has many dimensions, and each will require research and deliberation. Our five steps, however, provide a direction. They are the thought structure designed to spur the creativity of those who will put into place the first economics of fulfillment systems.

9

Education

A S OUR DISCUSSION ON economics of fulfillment systems and their implementation has made clear, the responsibility for economic function rests with the members of the economy. Our economy cannot operate and expand without its members understanding how the economy works and without its members conducting their economic affairs in light of that knowledge. To assure that those in the economy have the knowledge to conduct their economic activities in an enlightened way, our economy must incorporate an *educational system*. In this chapter, we explore the philosophy behind such a system and outline its structure and implementation.

We begin by delving into the nature of learning and education. What does it mean to learn, to teach? How do we acquire or communicate a skill or concept? How do we advance our understanding or further the knowledge held by another?[1]

Most of us think that an instructor's job is to "teach" his or her students. We believe that an instructor transfers ideas and skills into the minds and bodies of his or her pupils. To many people, this notion of education and of the role of the teacher forms the basis of educational theory. But when we look at education from the standpoint of our evolution of consciousness view of the universe, we realize that it is a more intriguing endeavor.

To glimpse the nature of this endeavor, we will use ourselves as an example. Throughout the book, we have grappled with many new ideas. Its reading may have been the first time we were exposed to notions such as the universe's nature is as an evolution of consciousness, socialism and

---

1. See *Book 1, Evolution of Consciousness*, chapters 9, 10, and 11.

capitalism are obsolete economic ideologies, and the role of the teacher is not to teach, at least as we normally think of teaching. When we face a new concept, we go through a process of internalizing it. We ponder the thought, consider it, learn more about it. The wheels in our head spin as we devote mental energy to understanding the idea.

This process is natural, unavoidable. And it tells us something about ourselves. We do not learn by directly inputting information. A computer uploads data into another computer, but this is nothing more than a duplication of binary expressions. Despite our infatuation with technology and notions of artificial intelligence, we do not behave like a computer. We do not process information in the same way. When we are exposed to a new idea, we ponder and grapple until we make it our own. Not even the best teacher can upload skills or knowledge to his or her pupils.

If we do not acquire information in a direct way, how do we learn a skill or concept? Here, also, the answer lies in our contemplative nature. If it is not in our makeup to achieve understanding without having to work at it, we are left with one alternative. We create understanding for ourselves. Through our pondering, through our grappling, we construct knowledge within ourselves. To learn is to create understanding. Through our trial, through our thought and reflection, we build the mental associations we need to grasp a new idea, to master a new skill. We are creative beings. Learning is a creative process.

As such, we no longer see the teacher as a conveyor of information but as a facilitator. The instructor's job is to nurture the student's ability to create understanding. The teacher guides the unfolding of creativity in his or her students. To teach is to show the way. To teach is to interact with the creative process of another to enable that person to create for him or herself a desired level of skill or knowledge.

In a moment, we will see how the above insight into learning and teaching relates to our economics of fulfillment educational ideals and methods. Before we delve into the educational theories and practices of tomorrow, however, it would be useful to look at the educational theories and practices of today. In most nations, we have grown up to believe that education serves lofty goals. We go to school to become enlightened leaders and citizens. We are told that education allows us to live to our potential and to contribute to the human community. In certain respects, contemporary education aspires to these objectives, or at least there are those in education who believe that it does and who strive to live up to these ideals in their work. But beyond rhetoric and the standards to which some educators hold themselves, we find the underlying nature of today's educational philosophy. Modern educational practices are based on a materialistic, scarcity derived, Darwinian interpretation of the human being and of the individual's role in society—the same limited understanding of the world on which we base contemporary economic practices. In this respect, education serves two purposes: First, it prepares us to occupy a place in society. Second, it prepares us to function in whatever form of economics society may embrace.

For a society to be a society, its members must know how to act and behave. In part, the objective of contemporary educational systems is to teach us to fit in. In some societies, the scope of education in this respect is limited to the basics of conduct, with the majority of social skills taught by parents and family. In other societies—in particular in more collective societies such as in present day Cuba and North Korea—education is dominated by social indoctrination. The goal is to graduate students who act, talk, and think alike and in an acceptable way.

In the minds of some, the greatest failing of educational systems in the supposedly open societies of Europe and the United States is the degree to which in recent years the emphasis has shifted from core subjects and open discourse to social indoctrination. Math, science, and history—topics the individual must know to form his or her own opinions—have to an increasing extent been replaced by politically sanctioned subjects. A class on global-warming may fulfill a science requirement, but it is no substitute for classes on physics, chemistry, and paleontology. A class on free-form art may fulfill a humanities requirement, but it is no substitute for classes on Middle Age architecture and Renaissance sculpture. A class on gay, ethnic, or woman's studies may fulfill a social science requirement, but it is no substitute for classes on the rise and fall of Ancient Egypt, Ancient Greece, and Ancient Rome, on the evolution of economics and the function of socialism and capitalism.

Particularly disturbing the last couple of decades is an emphasis on group work and social conformity at the expense of individual achievement. Inspired by a teamwork trend popularized by business schools during the 1980s—and for the most part abandoned by business when executives realized how little creativity and initiative a committee generates—education clings to the idea. The ability to work with others is essential; so is the ability to work alone. It is the Alexanders, the Caesars, the Newtons, the Napoleons, the Curries, the Fords, and the Einsteins who have advanced civilization, not the government task force on this or that. In addition to being able to work with others, we must be taught to question, to challenge, to think critically—to think for ourselves.

In this regard, one of the most neglected and most essential topics is history. In the United States, history, per say, is not generally taught below the college level but lumped into a "social studies" curriculum where it is dealt with superficially at best. Even in college, history requirements are minimal and most classes are taken as electives. In recent years, the history of Western civilization has been particularly neglected. With the advent of urbanization, the Middle East led humanity's ascent for thousands of years. Marked by the rise of Ancient Greece, however, the leading arrow of cultural evolution shifted across the Mediterranean. Societies in Africa and in the Far East, Near East, Middle East, and New World contributed to civilization's ascent and entwined with those of the West, but social, economic, technological, and governmental advance was centered in that region. To neglect the teaching of history and in particular that of Western civilization—including the American revolution, the American Civil War, and the values and beliefs that fueled these struggles—is to deny the student the perspective to deal with contemporary issues. To envision where we are headed, we must know where we have been.

To an increasing extent, educators have chosen to reinforce politically sanctioned values and topics—notions and subject matter a student grounded in science, history, and the core subjects of reading, writing, and mathematics, and thus empowered to think for him or herself, may not choose to embrace.

From the standpoint of the second major objective of contemporary education, that of economics, school systems in the United States and most developed nations are factories that spit-out the human component of global commerce—the labor part of land, labor, and capital.

Throughout our school years, the system propels us through standardized subjects. It measures our performance against that of our peers and established levels of achievement as it pits us in a competition for the economic doors we are led to believe our success will open. Administrators calculate our progress as they weigh the output of educational production against its cost in an attempt to satisfy government regulation, minimize political concern, and maximize the monetary efficiency of the knowledge machine. At each phase of our education, we are tested and advanced as the system prepares us to enter the work force.

Illustrative of the mechanistic nature of contemporary education is the concept of grades. Parents, teachers, and politicians assign a great deal of importance to grades. What would a student's life be like without his or her report card? But even the most conservative educators concede that grades provide no more than a superficial measure of a student's potential and contribute almost nothing to a student's motivation to learn. Rather, the value we place on grades is a measure of the degree to which we embrace our materialistic worldview. Grades allow companies and institutions to operate in the Darwinian mode of global economics, to select students for admission and employment and thus to lock students into the framework of winning and losing. Companies hire and fire to maximize labor output. Professions limit entry to create scarcity and bid up the price of services.

Our Darwinian approach to education has had a predictable outcome. On one hand, there are those students who thrive in the system, those who learn to adapt to its demands and to manipulate its requirements and as a result reap its benefits. On the other hand, there are those students who are left behind—men and woman who find it difficult to conform, who do not mesh with the gears of the educational mechanism. A 2008 study funded by America's Promise Alliance and the Bill and Melinda Gates Foundation reports that in the United States seventeen out of the nation's fifty largest cities had high school graduation rates lower than fifty percent.[2]

In the same way that society views the human being with respect to the economic machine, society views the student with respect to the educational machine. We are a cog in the works, a component in an educational contrivance designed to instill the value of economic conformity and output the product of labor.

Contemporary education is an industrial and governmental process put into place by a human community that has only begun to evolve beyond the scarcity-based views and ideals that for centuries have driven the advance of civilization. We can see this in the way we fund schools. We pay for education privately and socialistically. To us, today, education is an investment with a future social, economic, and ideological return.

2. Swanson, Christopher B., *Cities in Crisis: A Special Analytic Report on High School Graduation*, 2008.

The educational systems of the future, however, will not be centered on political conformity. Neither will they embrace traditional ideas of competition and revolve around measures of performance that support the Darwinian notion of selection for the best. In this respect, our economics of fulfillment educational philosophy represents the antitheses of contemporary educational philosophy. For an economics of fulfillment system to work—for us to function as individuals and as citizens of future cities, states, and nations—we must have the opportunity to learn what excites us in life and to acquire the skills we need to direct our creative energy toward that end.

Specifically, our educational ideology must emphasize creativity, individuality, and freedom of thought. As important, it must provide the student with the knowledge tools to pursue his or her passion and the base of understanding to reflect on and critically examine his or he place in the economy and in the human community.

To achieve these objectives, our economics of fulfillment educational system must expose the student to a diverse range of subjects and instill in the student the value to try this or that avenue. It is our right and obligation to navigate new paths of thought and experience, and our educational system must provide for this right and obligation. Moreover, our educational system must drive home the idea that we can always invent a better way to do things. Our students learn to challenge existing theories and approaches when we challenge existing theories and approaches. It is the teacher's job to invoke knowledge. It is also the teacher's job to confront that knowledge. We must break it down, figure out how it works, explore the thought behind it, define the assumptions on which it is based. In this way, the student learns to probe and question, to confront entrenched concepts and approaches.

In addition, our educational system must provide the student with skills specific to his or her interests. A homebuilder needs to learn how to calculate the load on beams and pillars. A doctor needs to learn how to diagnose disease and prescribe medications. A farmer needs to learn how to predict weather and growth cycles. A clothing designer needs to learn how to design styles and select fabrics. A sand and gravel provider needs to learn how to determine rock types and interpret geological strata. The knowledge tools we need to participate in our economy are diverse. To function, our economy needs engineers and architects, nurses and physicians, scientists and researchers, teachers and philosophers. We need men and women of all callings, and our educational system must provide the educational resources to pursue what by our personal mission in life we are driven to achieve.

Our educational system must also provide us with the understanding we need to reflect on our personal mission in life—to internalize and to come to terms with our place in the world. To do this, our educational system must instill in the student a foundation of knowledge that spans the academic disciplines: physics, chemistry, and mathematics, genetics, biology, and the earth sciences, history, politics, and economics, music, literature, and the humanities. Such a base of knowledge frees the mind to ponder in the deepest way, to question and challenge with the greatest wisdom and perspective. Though we will invariably be drawn to one discipline or another and focus our leaning on that end, to maximize our specialization we must be exposed to thought across the knowledge spectrum. Only with a diverse background to anchor our reflection can we form truly meaningful opinions and conclusions.

The economics of fulfillment educational philosophy is an expression of individual freedom, a system of beliefs that embodies our need for and our right to obtain the knowledge tools necessary to accept responsibility for and to make the most out of our place in society, the economy, and the human experience.

Moreover, to maximize our personal role in society and the human community, our educational philosophy must not only address the needs of the child and young adult developing his or her interests but also the needs of the man and woman of all ages who wishes to direct his or her creative energy in a new direction.

Say that after constructing houses for a few years our builder decides that construction is no longer his thing in life. His dreams and interests have evolved, and construction no longer serves as a medium for his personal growth. It is no longer his passion. Imagine he has taken a liking to healthcare and decides to become a doctor. In today's scarcity-based economic environment, this career change would be traumatic, wrought with the threat of financial ruin and the uncertainty of college and medical school admission. For our builder, it is a time of joy and renewal. As long as our builder achieves the background to grasp what he is taught in medical school, our educational system—by virtue of its economics of fulfillment idealism—must guarantee admittance. As long as our builder learns how to successfully treat patients, he will graduate. If our colleges

96

and universities cannot handle the number of students open access brings, we build more. In the economics of fulfillment world of tomorrow, taxes, tuition, and budgets have no meaning. Those who are driven to teach become teachers. Those who are driven to practice medicine become doctors, nurses, and emergency medical technicians. Those who are driven to build colleges and universities become engineers and architects. So what if there is an abundance of teachers. The teacher has more time to spend with the student. So what if there is an abundance of doctors. The doctor can get to know the patient. So what if there is an abundance of engineers and architects. Buildings will not fall down in earthquakes, and designs will not reflect the aesthetics of a scarcity-based world.

In the economics of fulfillment community of tomorrow, we will no longer think of school as something we as children and young adults participate in to fit into society. To an extent we can scarcely visualize today, we will integrate education into society. Education will be available to us as needed, at life's every crossroad.

This brings us to our final point concerning our economics of fulfillment educational philosophy. How does our ideology and the systems we create for its implementation address the issue that is so often at the center of educational rhetoric—the basics? The knowledge tools we need to function in our economy are diverse. As basic and varied as these skills may be, however, they have a foundation: reading, writing, and mathematics.

But in our economics of fulfillment system, students will not learn to read, write, and calculate to pass an exam. Instructors may use exams to measure our skill and to tune their interaction, but exams do not align our needs with our interests, that is unless our interest is to earn a good score on the exam. When we are driven to pursue our passion, we are driven to learn the skills we need and the reading, writing, and mathematics on which they rest. From a philosophical standpoint, this turns the way we teach basic skills upside-down.

Today, schools establish a foundation of reading, writing, and mathematics and encourage the student to follow the path their grades in these skills suggest is suited. To a degree, such an approach is necessary. The youngest students will start their education with spelling, penmanship, and addition and subtraction. But, in the future, we will not bog the student down in years of basic education. Instead—and at every practical level intermeshed with the nuts-and-bolts of education—we will encourage the student to discover and pursue their interests and by doing so nurture their motivation to learn the basic skills. We will then merge these skills into the student's curriculum and make available the resources he or she needs to fully develop them.

Take mathematics. In the United States, contemporary schools stretch mathematical education from the lowest grade through college. By the sixth grade, students are expected to perform basic arithmetic. By the ninth grade, students who have shown an aptitude for math and who advance in the field are expected to learn algebra, geometry, and trigonometry. In high school, students who have completed these courses are introduced to calculus with the majority of calculus training and that of statistics, linear algebra, and higher math reserved for college. Some students learn well with this approach. Many, however, find it too abstract and as a consequence turn away from math and never achieve the depth of study to appreciate and benefit from the discipline.

As mathematicians characterize it, mathematics is a language that allows us to precisely express the relationship between measurable quantities. In English, we would say that two sides of a rectangle are longer than the other two. In the language of mathematics, we would say that two sides of a rectangle are a specific distance longer than the other two, a geometry problem. In English, we would say that our car accelerates. In the language of mathematics, we would say that its velocity changes at a certain rate with respect to time, a calculus problem. In English, we would say that an electron spins around an atomic nucleus. In the language of mathematics, we would say that the electron has a certain likelihood of being at a certain location at a certain time, a probability problem. Like any language, mathematics influences the way we see our world. Mathematics is an empowering skill. It gives us the freedom to understand and to interact with our world in ways we would not otherwise enjoy.

In traditional education, we learn computational skills at an early age and only later, usually in college science and engineering courses, apply these skills. Rather than spend years learning long division and how to figure square roots, how much better it would be to incorporate within this study of the arithmetic of mathematics the meaning of mathematics. In the economics of fulfillment schools of tomorrow, we will expose the student at an early age to the framework of the mathematical language, to the beauty and usefulness of the mathematical system of expression. With this philosophical foundation in place, the student has the background to fully explore their interests. Their development, in turn, establishes the student's motivation to learn their math. If our passion is to design a park or a garden, a bridge or a skyscraper, or for that matter a video game or a skateboard ramp, we are driven to learn the arithmetic, algebra, geometry, trigonometry, and calculus that make it possible for us to realize our passion. We then provide the student with the resources he or she needs to immerse him or herself in the computational skills. There is no better way to learn our math than when we have a meaningful application.

To a greater extent than we do today, we will structure the learning environment in which we teach reading, writing, and mathematics to channel the student's natural motivation to learn. However we may implement the teaching of the basics, however, it is only with their command that we can acquire the knowledge to discover our passion in life and to direct our creative energy toward its resolution.

The objective of contemporary educational philosophy is social and economic conformity. The objective of our economics of fulfillment educational philosophy is social and economic prosperity, realized through individual growth and through freedom of thought and expression. To achieve this end, we must creatively build on and discard the old to create the new. Drill, discipline, core subjects, and many other traditional aspects of education are essential teaching tools. Children in particular need a structured learning environment. We as educators must also be open to new ideas: to exploration and experimentation. We must create a learning environment that nurtures our ability to teach and by doing so nurtures the student's ability to create understanding. Our aim is to provide the knowledge tools the student needs to figure things out for him or herself and, by doing so, to prepare the student to create a place in society and a place in the economy.

With this sketch of our economics of fulfillment educational philosophy in mind, we will bring the chapter to its conclusion with a look at how we will put our philosophy into place. We are members of the first economics of fulfillment economy. What must we do to create an economics of fulfillment educational system?

As did the nurse, farmer, builder, and clothing designer in last chapter's example, every member of our economy has the opportunity to pursue their interests. Among us will be those driven to teach—those who fulfill their creative needs through interaction with the student. By design, our economic system assures that only people with a passion for education enter the field. These people will be the force behind its implementation. They will teach the courses and establish the schools. They will implement our educational philosophy in the classroom.

Practicality suggests that this will take place on many levels. As educators, we will teach classes for adults and classes for children. Kids and adults learn differently, embrace different things as important and meaningful. As we do today, we must design programs that maximize the learning potential of each group. Also, like today, classes will be centered on levels and topics. The creative process advances progressively. We learn complex ideas by building on simple ideas. Levels and topics will continue to be a part of education, though as our mathematics example illustrated we may implement learning progressions in different ways. Along these lines, schools and teachers will coordinate their programs. Some schools will be small, a single instructor teaching a single subject. Others will be as large as contemporary colleges and universities.

Unlike today, however, our schools will not be socially and geographically isolated. Present schools are discrete entities within the community. Life on and off campus is different. In the future, we will integrate education into the community. To a greater extent than today, students will work in and take courses offered by industry. Accordingly, those in industry will take and offer courses at schools. In many ways, the economics of fulfillment community in its entirety will be a university—one integrated into every aspect of life.

The steps to implementing our educational system, then, break down as follows: First, those with a passion for teaching will prepare themselves to teach. They will acquire an understanding of educational philosophy and a background in the topics they wish to instruct. Second, teachers will offer classes and create schools. This will take place in much the same way that an individual forms a business. To a greater extent than today, schools in the future will be independently run rather than administered through a government bureaucracy. Education will be managed from the bottom up rather than from the top down—the teacher driven by his or her own ideals, objectives, and sense of mission and not be funds, unions, mandates, and legislatures. We will create and reinvent our schools and curriculums as we need and desire. Third, those in education will coordinate their activities with industry and with one another to meet the needs of the community and to inspire us to pursue our interests.[3] We will teach classes, open schools, and incorporate existing educational resources as needed to establish a social and economic environment conducive to learning and to maximizing our potential as educators, and by doing so the potential of every student.

In our economics of fulfillment economy, education and creativity go hand-in-hand. In the future, we will not graduate from school and move on. Education will be a part of our existence, available to us at every age and at every turn in life's path. Education will be the nexus of our personal evolution, the driving center that allows us to further the evolution of the human community. Just as we must have freedom to evolve, our educational system must have freedom to evolve. The structure of our system reflects our state of mind. Today, education is rigid, centrally controlled, the creative freedom of the teacher limited by politics and bureaucracy. In the future, education will be open, flexible, and inspiring. Teachers will be free to shape their educational practices to provide the wisdom we need to further our evolutionary journey. The teacher will become a dominant force in the universe's advance, the professional that nurtures our social and personal evolution.

3. See chapter 10, *Government*.

10

Government

THROUGHOUT OUR DISCUSSION ON implementing the first economics of fulfillment systems, we have emphasized the importance of individual responsibility. Our economy cannot function without the members of the economy taking it on themselves to understand how the economy works. Neither can our economy function without the members of the economy taking it on themselves to determine how they can structure their creative activities to allow the economy to operate in a way that allows everyone to fulfill their material and higher needs. This, however, is not to imply that our economy is free of all forms of central organization. In the last chapter, we described the educational system that will allow our newly founded economic community to thrive. In this chapter, we describe the governing structures it needs to flourish.

To do so, we begin by exploring the nature of government. We all like, dislike, turn to, and turn away from government. But what does government mean? What is government about? How has government changed over time and how does this change relate to the trends we previously established concerning the evolution of the individual, the evolution of economics, and the evolution of social structure?

The textbook definition of government goes something like this: Government is a political organization made up of individuals and institutions sanctioned to make policies and to conduct affairs of state. We empower government to regulate the activities of people within the territory of our nation or within that of our jurisdiction and to control the dealings of those in our nation or jurisdiction with outside political entities. To better understand the textbook definition of government and to lay the groundwork for the redefinition of government economics of fulfillment makes possible, a brief history is in order.

Government existed as far back as the early hunting and gathering cultures, or however far back one draws the line. It was not until urbanization and the scarcity it created, however, that government attained the dominance we normally associate with its dealings. In the empires of Sumer, Egypt, Assyria, Persia, and Macedonia, individuals with absolute power ruled—despots whose will was to be followed without question. Not long after these empires, less autocratic forms of government emerged in the city-states of Greece, in particular in Athens and Corinth. In these communities, the rule of law predominated, and rulers and officials were to a greater extent than in the past responsible to the citizens who chose or supported them.

The city-states of Greece, and those of Asia Minor influenced by the Greeks, provided the material for the political theories of Plato and Aristotle. Plato's ideas about government are articulated in his treatise the *Republic*, a discussion on justice and the class structure of the state. Aristotle's views, and in particular his system of classifying states, have also been influential. Aristotle defined good governments as those that serve the general welfare and bad governments as those that serve the individuals in power. In this framework, he distinguished three categories of government: monarchy, or government by a single individual; aristocracy, government by a select few; and democracy, government by many. Later philosophers defined additional classes of government: tyranny, or rule by an individual in his or her own interest; oligarchy, or rule by a few in their own interest; and ochlocracy, or mob rule. Other categories include theocracy, or rule by religious leaders, and bureaucracy, or rule by administrative officials.

Ancient Rome, which evolved from a city-republic to become an empire, also influenced the development of government. Among Rome's many achievements was the principle of constitutional law. This principle established the law of the state as superior to the law of lower governing bodies, such as the enactments of a city or regional legislature. The Roman Catholic Church kept alive this idea, known as the concept of "universal dominion," during the Middle Ages, an action that helped to create the city-republics of Italy and the commercial city-states of Europe that formed the trade alliance known as the Hanseatic League.

The nation as we think of it today emerged as a governing form in the sixteenth century, brought about by economic factors and by the Reformation. In the first nation-states, the power of the reigning monarch was unlimited, exemplified by the aphorism of King Louis XIV of France: *L'état, c'est moi,* "I am the state." In time, the demand of the bourgeoisie, or middle class, for constitutional and representative government challenged the power of the monarchs. In England, the Glorious Revolution in 1688 established the preeminence of Parliament; and, a century later, the American Revolution, beginning in 1775, and the French Revolution, beginning in 1789, gave rise to the modern democratic movement.

In the nineteenth century, democratic ideals strengthened; and, in the twentieth century, the growing political power of the masses led to an expansion in the scope of government. Government not only served as a means of central control but also took on the responsibility for education, social security, scientific research, and conservation of natural resources. Between 1945 and 1951, the Labour party of Great Britain nationalized many industries. Earlier in the century, the first communist states and modern totalitarian governments emerged, notably the Union of Soviet Socialist Republics.

As the textbook says, government is a political structure empowered to regulate the activities of people within a jurisdiction and to control their dealings with outside entities. In this respect, government is a means of *central control.* Government regulates economic activity and human behavior. Through the body of laws and the police and military institutions government maintains, it mandates rights and responsibilities.

Government also administers *social services.* The extent to which it does so varies from nation to nation. Some countries strongly embrace this form of socialism. Based on the theory of wealth redistribution through taxation, their goal is to assure their citizenry an education and a reasonable standard of living. Others nations provide only enough resources to those in need to placate the population and maintain the stability of the government. To prevent anarchy in Ancient Rome after the burning of the city, Emperor Nero gave free grain to those on the streets.

The role of government as a regulatory force and the role of government as a mechanism to administer social services are well studied. Government, however, has a less apparent role and meaning. It is a *manifestation of social structure.*[1] As we have described, over the course of evolution, social structure has become less collective. The human community has integrated into more nestled and strongly bonded social ar-

1. See *Book 1, Evolution of Consciousness,* chapters 5, 9, 11, and 12.

rangements. As does every organization, a social body represents a level of consciousness—an awareness greater than the consciousness embodied in its members. This is not to say that a society has greater worth or significance than an individual; a society is the expression of the relationships maintained between individuals. Greater social unity is the outcome of greater personal individuality, but a society is an entity in itself. It has an identity of its own. In this, we find the essence of nationalism and patriotism. When we feel patriotic, we feel we are part of something that is greater than ourselves: that we belong, that we have a greater purpose in life. In addition to its overt roles, government reflects the unity of the citizenry. Government is a manifestation of social structure.

As a manifestation of social structure, government functions as a *coordinating mechanism*. Government provides the organizational framework to undertake large public works projects and to wage large-scale conflicts. Without a governing structure, the Egyptians could not have built the pyramids, the Romans could not have built the aqueducts, the allies could not have defeated Nazi Germany, and the Americans could not have put a man on the moon. Government allows us to accomplish objectives that are too big to undertake on our own.

In summary, contemporary government has four major roles: the imposition of central control, the providing of social services, the manifestation of social organization, and the coordination of public projects. Based on this expanded definition of government, history takes on a new dimension: We can add government to the evolutionary trends we have established. As the individual evolved to greater autonomy, society evolved from more to less collective forms. Corresponding to this complexification of social structure, economic systems evolved from structures that provided a great deal of central control and little individual freedom to structures that provided less central control and greater individual freedom. As *Figure 9* illustrates, government also changed in response to our needs, expectations, and view of the world. Government evolved from autocratic forms, with power centered in the hands of a few, to *democratic* forms, with power increasingly distributed among the masses.

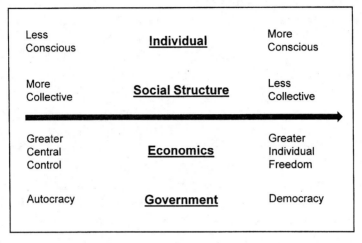

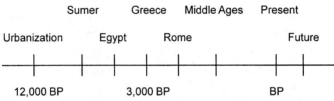

Fig. 9. Government Trend. As human society evolved from more to less collective forms, and economic systems evolved from systems with greater central control and less individual freedom to systems with less central control and greater individual freedom, government evolved from autocratic to democratic forms.

This introduces the topic of democracy and brings us to a definition that the reader may not have come across in the textbooks. The more collective the society, the less the value of the individual and the less democratic the government. The less collective the society, the greater the value of the individual and the more democratic the government. Democracy from the Greek *dēmokratiā*—meaning *dēmos*, or people, and *kratos*, or rule—is not a static form of government defined by the vote or by such devices as a constitution and a bill of rights. Democracy represents a spectrum, a measure of the individual's freedom to participate in government administration.

This definition is readily apparent in the complex social and governmental structures of today. In our global community, democracy has become the dominant governing form. Most nations embrace, are on the road to embracing, or claim to be on the road to embracing democratic ideals. Our definition of democracy as a spectrum of the individual's ability to participate in government implies that we can carry out democracy in different ways and to different extents. Democracy in Great Britain and the United States is more open to public input than democracy in India and Mexico, which is more open to public input than democracy in Russia and Venezuela. In Iraq, former president Saddam Hussein was periodically reelected president by what was propagandized to be a unanimous vote. Not only were citizens required to participate in the election and had no choice but to vote for him, he went so far as to on occasion require voters to sign their ballots in their own blood. The extent to which democracy manifests reflects the evolutionary level of the underlying society.

As does the way in which we implement democracy. In Ancient Greece and Rome, individuals spoke their mind in public forums. They were free to voice their opinions, and rulers were free to listen or not. We, today, speak our mind in books, television, and on the Internet, and leaders are free to listen or not. Throughout history, people have expressed their opinions in rallies and marches and by forming political groups to take up their causes. In the traditional sense, we implement democracy through the vote.

In this regard, nations employ two methods of practice. The first is democracy through *direct vote*. In this approach, citizens vote for or against a specific measure. Should the city issue bonds to pay for the construction of a school, yes or no? Should the state government legalize physician assisted suicide, yes or no? Should the state government impose a gas tax to pay for roads and bridges, yes or no? In a direct vote, we vote for or against something, and our vote counts toward the outcome. The result with a majority wins—however we may define majority. By way of the direct vote, the individual imposes his or her views on government.

The direct vote involves the citizen in a personal way; but, to steer government in the best direction, the voter must understand what he or she is voting for. Most of us do not have the time or information to sort through the issues. For this reason, governments also practice democracy through elected leadership—*representative democracy*. Rather than vote for or against a measure, we vote for an individual whom we entrust to understand or learn about the issues and to enact legislation in our interest. To further assure that our representatives have our interests at heart, we limit their power. In the United States, the President, the Senate, and the House of Representatives share power, which is further limited by the courts. In a representative democracy, or a *republic*, we build checks and balances into the political process.

In this regard, we must remember that the vote, direct or representative, is not democracy but a tool to implement democracy. As such, it can be misused. A majority opinion, for example, can compel the exile or imprisonment of an out-of-favor political minority. Similarly, what would prevent a majority from taxing a minority and voting itself perks from the treasury. To prevent situations like this, democratic governments must embrace values and ideals that are superior to the mechanisms of democracy—that embody the ideal of democracy, as at the time a society defines it. A constitution, for example, may be employed to establish the role, limits, and procedures of government. A bill of rights, which in the United States is contained in the first ten amendments to the Constitution, may be employed to establish certain individual privileges as inalienable, as based in *natural law*, or law of God and human nature, as opposed to *positive law*, or law of man.

This brings us to the issue of democracy as we practice it today. Do we appropriately use the democratic mechanism of the vote? In the larger sense, does government in the United States and other developed nations allow the individual to participate in a meaningful way?

In addition to the obvious consideration of a free election, for democracy to function it must meet certain criteria. First, we and our representatives must as much as possible understand the issues. We must have the information we need to make sound decisions. Second, we and our representatives must have the interests of society at heart. Our motivations must go beyond personal gain and embrace a higher social good. And, third, we and our representatives must be able to look beyond daily tasks and issues. As citizens and leaders, we must have a vision of the future—an understanding of where we as a society are at and an ideal of where we as a society want to be. If this or any of our criteria is not met, the population does not contribute to government in a meaningful way. We may hold elections and embrace the mechanisms of democracy but our votes and activities do not impact government to the extent our leaders may want us to believe.

In today's world, political factions, corporations in particular but also other groups, wield a great deal of power. In Washington DC, for example, one of the most powerful lobbies is the environmental movement, which has successfully stopped the expansion of nuclear energy and offshore drilling. This concentration of power has an unavoidable consequence. In our politically driven world, those with power will invariably choose to exercise their power for the benefit of their agenda and for the detriment of competing agendas.

By virtue of the vote and a government's legal and police institutions, democracy pools the power of the citizen, who has little alone, to mediate the actions of economic and other concerns for the greater good of society and the individual. This places political factions in opposition to government. Thus, to achieve their goals, factions work to manipulate government. Masked in the rhetoric of free-market, environmental, or other ideology, those with power go to whatever lengths are necessary to secure the government's backing of their objectives.

It follows that for a corporation or other interest to manipulate government, it must control the process that empowers government—the democratic process. We cannot go back in time to where in most nations we will stand for autocratic rule. Those in our society with power cannot apply their power directly. A corporation cannot stage a coup and appoint an employee prime minister, at least not in a stable nation. Corporations, environmental, and other interests must control government subtly, covertly, through the back door, by manipulating the democratic process.

To do this, they corrupt the criteria a democracy must uphold to function. Capital is power. The tool of corruption is money. Economic, environmental, and other concerns spend vast sums to limit our access to information and, by doing so, to center-stage issues and to steer votes in a desired direction. Multinational corporations own or back the world's news organizations. Politicians and the public relations firms they hire boil complex problems down to slogans and promises. Environmental groups manipulate the media and legal system and hire celebrities to appeal to our sense of what is "good" for the Earth with no regard for the complexity of environmental issues.[2] In the end, we vote our pocketbook or based on our emotional response to an issue, and our representatives support the groups and causes that fund their political ambitions. As for the vision that will guide us into the future, what chance is there for a person inspired by a vision other than a politically left or right version

---

2. See *Book 3, Blueprint for Reconstruction*, chapter 4.

of the status quo to survive the political process? To paraphrase United States President George Herbert Walker Bush in the late 1980s: "I'm not big on the vision thing."

When we fail to uphold the criteria a democracy needs to function, we do not have government where we as individuals contribute in a meaningful way. We have government by those with power for those with power. Is this what we see in democratic nations today? Environmental and animal rights groups block forest and wildlife management and, in the United States, have limited the production of nuclear energy, restricted the drilling for gas and oil, and placed severe limits on the use of coal.[3] Governments bail out bankrupt corporations but fail to fund basic services. Scarcely a day goes by without word of a scandal over misuse of government funds or over political ties between business and government: bank fiascos, insurance fiascos, accounting fiascos, mutual-fund fiascos, real-estate fiascos. In the 1990s, the electrical utility industry in the western United States promised lower electric bills and legislators approved utility deregulation. The result, blackouts, staggering utility costs, and soaring corporate profits. Do we have democracy or do we maintain the facade of democracy? Is democracy as we practice it today a viable concept for the future or, as society continues its rise from collectivity, will we demand a yet more open democratic form?

With this assessment of democracy as it is today practiced in Europe, the United States, and most developed nations, we refocus our eyes and look ahead in time. What will government be like and how will we practice democracy in our economics of fulfillment community?

As we have pointed out, present government has four roles: central control, social services, social structure, and coordination of activities. In today's world, central control is the dominant function, with, in many nations, the administration of social services occupying a disproportionate share of government resources. Government invokes our patriot desires when it serves a political interest and engages in public works to address security, transportation, and other matters; but, though important, these roles are secondary. Above all, government manages the economy and funds social programs, which is a form of economic management.

In our economics of fulfillment community, companies do not compete for survival. There are no competitive forces to manipulate and no

---

3. Ibid., chapters 4 and 9.

need for a governing body to oversee such manipulation. Our economic model also eliminates the need for government-sponsored social services. When every member of the economy has access to capital, every member has the resources he or she needs to go about their lives and contribute to the economy. We end disparities of wealth and opportunity and eliminate the need for socialistic wealth redistribution. By its nature, economics of fulfillment makes obsolete the principle functions of contemporary government. It ends the need for centrally controlled economic management and for tax funded social programs.

This shifts the balance between governmental roles to social structure and coordination of creative energy. Here the nature of government aligns with the way we will implement government in our economics of fulfillment community. Thus far, our discussion on economic implementation has focused on steps, on procedures to establish economic structures. We will not create government in this way. We will not put government into place; government will arise as a manifestation of our evolving social needs, where and to the extent needed.

Take our homebuilder. He needs construction resources and information. He also needs a forum to share his knowledge. As such, our builder is part of a community of builders. He may be a citizen of a state or nation or a member any number of other groups; but, by virtue of his profession and his passion in life, he is also a member of a builder's society. Motivated by the need to align their creative efforts, builders will establish a governing body that reflects the social structure of their community and that allows them to coordinate and maximize their creative activities. The same can be said of bankers, farmers, teachers, and clothing designers. It can also be said of state, national, and international social organizations. In the future, there will also be a level of world government, but unlike socialist-capitalistic notions of world government today, sometimes referred to as the "new world order," the role of government will not be central control. In whatever form and to whatever extent world government may manifest, it will arise in support of the individual. It will emerge from the bottom up as opposed to from the top down, imposed by a ruling elite. Governing bodies will form or evolve out of existing bodies in response to the individual's desire to be part of humanity's greater movement in evolution.

Government will also emerge in response to specific needs. One of the greatest challenges faced by the first economics of fulfillment systems will be to integrate new members into the economic fabric in a way that assures economic stability. What businesses must we incorporate to minimize our need for outside resources? What educational offerings must we provide to allow new members, born into a scarcity-based world, to function in a free economic environment? To a large extent, we will accomplish these objectives through private efforts. We will form schools and open businesses as our needs and interests dictate and to assist new members. Governing structures, however, will emerge where an overall administrative body is of value.

On a similar line, government will emerge to administer public works projects. In any society, certain economic activities are so large and so vital that they require an overall coordinating mechanism. No more fragmented airline industry, greed-driven utility industry, incoherent telecommunication system, and crumbling highway and railroad system. In our economics of fulfillment economy, we will create governing structures as needed to, in support of our private efforts, assure that we have basic services and a functional infrastructure.

Our ability to create government to achieve specific objectives changes the relationship between government and the citizen. No longer will government be removed from and above us, monitoring our every move. No longer will government be the tool of those with power to limit the freedom and harness the labor of those without power. As such, the tone of government will change. Like others in our economy, those in government will fulfill their creative needs by administering to the needs of the community. To an extent that is difficult to imagine today, government will be a partner in life, guiding and assisting as we strive to further our personal goals. The focus of government will shift from the political objectives of the present to the creative possibilities of the future. Government will demand and bring into its ranks men and women with vision.

The historical trend continues. Collective societies evolve into less collective societies. Centrally controlled economic systems evolve into free and open economic systems. Government evolves from autocratic forms to democratic forms. Today, we embrace a primitive, often corrupt, form of democracy—one where the individual has limited ability to influence leadership—the facade of democracy. In our economics of fulfillment community, we will embrace a new ideal of democracy. Whatever techniques we may adopt or devise to implement it, we will practice democracy where the freedom of the many is realized through the freedom of the individual—democracy as an expression of the open economy and the nestled and strongly bonded social structures we will form. Throughout history, government power has shifted from the few to the masses. As we implement economics of fulfillment, government power will shift from the masses to every individual.

In this section of the book, we focused on the practical aspects of the economics of fulfillment philosophy and concluded that the most reasonable way to implement the first economic systems based on that philosophy will be on a local level. We will form a bank, establish a startup fund, open businesses, conduct transactions, and put into place an information system. With these steps, we create the foundation to establish the educational system we need to support our economic goals. We also create the foundation that will allow the governing structures to manifest that express our sense of community and that enable us to further our creative objectives.

These ideas outline our transcendence beyond scarcity-based economics—beyond socialism and capitalism. They also bring us to our recognition of the deeper significance of the economics of fulfillment philosophy in humankind's evolution. The economic system through which we conduct our material affairs reflects our level of social organization, which reflects our level of individual freedom and internalization of the universe. As our drive for freedom and less collective social structure propels us forward in time, we will find our thoughts increasingly shifting to the implementation of an economics of fulfillment world. In this respect, economics of fulfillment is more than an economic philosophy.[4] It represents the next great stride in humankind's cultural evolution—the end to which socialism and capitalism and the scarcity-based worldview on which these ideologies are based must climax. In whatever form or forms it may manifest, economics of fulfillment is a dimension of evolution, an inescapable development in humankind's ascent. As such, economics of fulfillment takes on a profound role in the process of humanity's becoming—the function of evolutionary catalyst. Economics of fulfillment is the development that, as our look at the educational and governmental ideologies of tomorrow attests and as we will further describe in the book's next section, will open the way for human progress on a new and remarkably liberated level.

---

4. See *Book 1, Evolution of Consciousness*, chapter 14.

PART FOUR

Freedom

11

Money's End

W E BEGAN THIS BOOK with a chapter titled *Freedom*. Freedom is that which allows the human being to grow and evolve. Freedom is the environment of the creative process, the state of the universe where evolution can take place. Freedom is the desire that when fulfilled—and that through the action of its fulfillment—opens the way into our future. As the book progressed and we came to understand the economics of fulfillment philosophy, we realized that it is a system of beliefs structured to provide greater individual freedom than socialism, capitalism, and their contemporary variations. Economic freedom will define our future. Economic freedom will allow us to achieve our creative dreams. As we will see by the end of this section, our growing economic freedom will have an even more thought-provoking outcome. It will redefine economics in a way that goes so far as to surpass all that we have come to learn and invent about economics—so far as to surpass economics of fulfillment.

Of immediate impact on the outpouring of freedom poised to grip our world is the decline and collapse of socialism-capitalism and the emergence and spread of systems of economic practice based on the economics of fulfillment framework of beliefs. Where and in what conditions will the first economics of fulfillment systems take hold? How will we move beyond present economic practices and, when it comes to our use of the abstraction we call money that today pervades nearly every aspect of the human experience, to what outcome will it climax?

We begin with the question of Earth's geopolitical landscape. Defined by current political, economic, and geographical conditions, what nations and regions will be the first to contribute to the economics of fulfillment movement? Will the economic communities of the future have a geopolitical basis?

For an economics of fulfillment system to begin, certain conditions must be present. Above all, there must be a need. We must face a degree of economic uncertainty. The wealthy have no reason to change their way of life. For the upper economic classes, the world works. The wealthy are on top of the scarcity-based food chain. Unless members of this group are driven by ideology, and there are those who will be, the wealthy have no motivation to create the first economics of fulfillment systems. Also necessary for economic reformation is education. The founding members of our economy must understand current economic and business practices. They must also understand the economics of fulfillment ideology and embrace the assumptions and guiding principle on which it is based. They must know how to create a bank, to form companies, and to put into place an information system. One other factor must come into play. The founding members must have resources. They must have the ability to raise startup capital.

As restrictive as these conditions may seem, they open the way to many possible locations for the implementation of an economics of fulfillment model. Interestingly, the world's wealthiest nations may harbor the seed of economic reform. Although the richest nations have an upper class, most citizens in these nations are not members of this class. Most live from paycheck to paycheck, locked in a struggle to make ends meet and to build a better life for their families. The population of the wealthiest nations is also educated, with many trained in science, business, and economics. In addition, the population has access to startup resources. As individuals, we may not have much money, but we can pool our funds to raise startup capital. These points suggest that the first economics of fulfillment communities will emerge in the world's most stable and prosperous nations.

This, however, need not be the case. Nowhere is the need for economic reform more deeply felt than in the world's developing nations. Socialism and capitalism have failed to provide these nations with stable economic conditions. War and hunger ravage many countries, and multinational corporations and corrupt governments freely exploit labor and natural resources. The limiting factors in the developing world are the educational base and the availability of capital. But these factors may not be as significant as they seem. We can provide education through the economics of fulfillment framework. Initially, those who found an economic community need only put into place a system sufficient to instill basic skills and the knowledge needed to function in our economy. With this base established, the educational system can grow and diversify as it would in any economics of fulfillment community. The lack of capital may also be less important than we may think. Our startup fund must be large enough to allow our economy to interact with the surrounding economy. In an industrial nation, this amount would be substantial. In an agricultural nation, it would be less. If the nation had some form of a bartering system, there might be almost no need for hard currency. The developing nations have one other advantage. To a greater extent, they are free of the legal and regulatory structure that impedes business in the developed nations—in particular, politically motivated labor and environmental regulations as opposed to those with practical health and safety benefits.[1] These factors suggest that the first economics of fulfillment communities will spring up in the developing world.

One other scenario exists. Today's global economy is defined by the flow of capital across territorial boundaries and by the multinational corporation. Inspired by the notion of free trade, we can envision an economics of fulfillment community without geographical borders, one founded by members living throughout the world and that operates through the planet's electronic infrastructure. Such is an intriguing idea, and it may happen. But it will not be the general case. Our economy is an expression of societal evolution. Social structure need not be geographically based, but the roots of social structure lie in proximity. We thrive on face-to-face human interaction. Economic activity in the future will take place without regard to territory. Trade will be less restricted than the most liberal trade policies of today. But for the most part, economic communities will have a geographical basis.

So, where does this leave us? Conceivably, the first economics of fulfillment systems could spring up anywhere in the world, though we might argue that due to capital and educational resources the industrial nations have an advantage. Wherever the first economics of fulfillment communities begin, their founding will be driven by need. Their creation will be pursued by those who question tradition, yearn for a better life, and have the wisdom to build that life. The people of every nation and region have the potential to play a role in economic reformation.

---

1. See *Book 3, Blueprint for Reconstruction*, chapter 4.

With this said, it would be useful to narrow the scope of our discussion and look at certain situations that illustrate the conditions necessary for an economics of fulfillment system to take root. Though purely speculative, they spur the imagination and show us the diversity of circumstances able to spark economic rebirth.

The first of these situations expands on our look at economic reformation in the developing world. For nearly a century, humanitarian organizations have offered relief to people around the world faced with political unrest and with floods, droughts, and other natural hazards. We think of hurricanes and tidal waves, forest fires, civil wars, and despotic rulers. Nations such as Chad, Sudan, Burma, Bangladesh, and others come to mind.

Relief programs are run privately and by the United States and other stable governments. They are also run by the United Nations. On the political level, relief organizations, in particular those administered by the United Nations, are justifiably open to criticism. Bickering among leadership often overshadows the practical objective of humanitarian relief. Below the political level, however, tens of thousands of nurses, physicians, and other relief workers devote their lives to meeting the health and nutritional requirements of others. The adverse conditions in which many of these people work—administratively and on the ground—and the good they are able to accomplish in light of these conditions is a testament to the human spirit, a true embodiment of the economics of fulfillment ideal.

Still, though, relief always seems to be directed to the same locations. How many typhoons have devastated Bangladesh? How many battles have been waged between Muslims and Christians in North Africa? How many medal-boasting dictators have taken control of this or that country only to a few years later be overthrown by yet other medal-boasting dictators? No matter how much money and human effort the developed world pours into the undeveloped world, little seems to change. Education is still limited. Governments are still unstable. Houses in hurricane zones are still built out of wood. Houses in earthquake zones are still built out of unreinforced masonry bricks. Irrigation systems are still inadequate. Fertilizer is still rare and expensive. Tractors and farm equipment are still scarce. Water, sewage, electrical, and transportation systems are still dysfunctional.

Part of the blame for our lack of progress falls with militias, third-world governments, and other groups that siphon off foreign aid. Part of the blame falls with multinational corporations who have a vested interest in cheap land and labor. Part of the blame also falls with the politics of relief organizations. There are territorial disputes between agencies—turf wars over what one or another group may contribute in a particular region or toward a particular disaster. Relief organizations must also justify their existence. To stay in business, there must be a crop failure. There must be a damaging hurricane or a violent revolutionary uprising. For these and other reasons, organizations typically limit their relief to the immediate needs of subsistence. There are private organizations and groups such as the United States Peace Corps that work to educate populations in agricultural production and to instill the skills needed for self-sufficiency, but most relief efforts are limited to food, clothing, shelter, and healthcare.

Capitalism and socialism are ripe for abuse and corruption. Is economics of fulfillment the economic philosophy that will allow the world's relief organizations to do more than provide humanitarian services? Can relief agencies incorporate the economics of fulfillment ideal into their efforts? Can agencies employ an economics of fulfillment model to create self-sufficient economies, to move families out of poverty and into freedom and prosperity?

Our next situation for economic reformation is more sweeping. With regard to the conditions where economics of fulfillment can take root, one of the world's most powerful nations stands out as illustrative. It is a country with a heritage of peace and turmoil, of stagnation and transformation. The nation of interest is Russia.

As the independent republic we know today, Russia was established in the early 1990s. It is the largest country in the world, with twice the land area of the United States. On the north, Russia borders the Arctic Ocean. On the east, it borders the Pacific Ocean, the Bering Sea, and the Sea of Okhotsk. On the south, Russia borders China, Mongolia, Kazakhstan, Azerbaijan, Georgia, and the Black Sea. On the west, it borders Ukraine, Belarus, Latvia, Estonia, Finland, and Norway. With a population of 150 million, Russia ranks sixth in the world, after China, India, the United States, Indonesia, and Brazil. Russia contains one-half of the world's coal reserves, forty percent of the world's natural gas reserves, and a larger petroleum reserve than any other country. The nation also has major deposits of nickel, cobalt, tungsten, iron-ore, manganese, and molybdenum.

But it is not these characteristics that set Russia apart. It is its history. In the pre-Christian era, the territory that would become Russia was inhabited by nomadic tribes. In the north were the Slavs, the ancestors of the modern Russian people. In the south were a succession of Asian groups, including the Scythians, Cimmerians, and Sarmatians. In the early centuries of the Christian era, a succession of Slavic expansions displaced many Asian peoples and, in the ninth century, led to rule by the Scandinavian chief Vladimir the Great, who decreed Byzantine Christianity the official religion of the Russian people. This religion gave rise to the Russian Orthodox Church. In the Middle Ages, Russia became a federation of city-states, loosely aligned and often at war. In the early thirteenth century, the Mongol armies of Genghis Khan invaded, and it was not until the fourteenth century that Moscow led Russia from Tatar rule.

The eighteenth century saw the rise of imperialist Russia. Over the course of wars against Sweden and Prussia, Peter the Great reshaped Russia along Western European lines and established Russia as a European power. Catherine the Great furthered Peter's dreams of conquest and expansion. She turned her armies against the Ottoman Empire to acquire Black Sea ports and, in the Russo-Turkish War, acquired territory in the Crimea and Poland. Catherine was succeeded by her son Paul I, who was followed by his son, Alexander I, and by Nicholas I, Alexander II, and Alexander III.

In the late 1800s, Russia emerged through a succession of wars and attempts at social reform as a nation of censorship and police control. "Russification" programs led to the death and imprisonment of thousands of Jews and other minorities. As in Western Europe, industrialization had swept Moscow, St. Petersburg, and other cities. Sparked by deplorable working conditions, Marxist ideas inspired a revolutionary movement. In 1894, Nicholas II, eldest son of Alexander III, ascended the throne and increased oppression and police control. Inside Russia, there was an upsurge of terrorist acts. Outside Russia, Vladimir Lenin and other revolutionaries directed the Socialist movement.

In 1905, the priest Georgy Apollonovich Gapon marched demonstrators to the Winter Palace to present demands for reform. Imperial troops opened fire on the demonstrators, killing and wounding hundreds. Riots and strikes broke out. Soldiers deserted, and workers formed a council to lead a general strike. By 1906, the government had regained control. In 1914, World War I broke out, and military failures fueled a resurgence of revolutionary activities. In 1917, riots tore through Moscow. Troops refused to fire on demonstrators and joined the revolt. In March of that year, Nicholas II abdicated—to be slaughtered with his family in the cellar of the home where they had been detained—thus ending the Russian Empire and making way for the *Union of Soviet Socialist Republics*.

The absolute power of Lenin's successor Joseph Stalin, whose purges took the lives of more men and women than those of Hitler, brutally transformed the nation from an agrarian society into an industrial and technological giant. By the 1980s, nearly all Soviet citizens were literate, and Soviet society produced many of the world's top engineers and scientists. Despite corruption, vast inequalities of wealth, and pervasive shortages of goods and services, the Soviet Union enjoyed comparatively stable economic conditions. But those in power could not hold back the tide of evolution. They could not forestall the human drive to autonomy and less collective social structure. In 1991, the Soviet Union broke apart, and Russia emerged as a nation.[2]

The transition from socialism to capitalism was abrupt. For the first time in the memory of most Russians, citizens were without the stability of a planned economy. This situation was worsened by inaction on the part of the world community. In the years after World War II, the United States poured billions into rebuilding Japan and Europe. In certain respects, the collapse of the Soviet Union was the last battle of World War II. But the victors of this battle had no Martial Plan. Western Europe was preoccupied with reconstructing the Eastern Block and creating a European union. The United States had other interests at heart. An arm of multinational business, the United States government based its Russian policy on the belief that market forces and corporate interests would rebuild the Russian economy. The result was business exploitation and a society in a state of social and economic breakdown. The citizenry faced hunger, alcoholism, unemployment, and a failing healthcare system. Tuberculosis and other illnesses ravaged the countryside, and birth rates and life expectancy plummeted.

Yet, as tumultuous as the transition from socialism proved to be, capitalism freed the creative power of the individual to an extent not seen

2. The evolutionary trend toward less collective social forms was at the heart of the decline and fall of the Soviet Union. This evolutionary development, however, manifested through a number of political and economic actions and events. These involved the president of the United States, Ronald Reagan, the prime minister of Great Britain, Margaret Thatcher, the pope of the Roman Catholic Church, John Paul II, and the president of the Soviet Union, Mikhail Gorbachev, and centered on a massive military buildup by the United States. A plunge in the cost of crude oil, the Soviet Union's primary export and source of hard currency, also factored into the collapse.

in communist Russia. By the early years of the twenty-first century, energy and agricultural production had increased, and the government had initiated moves such as low tax rates to encourage investment and business startups. As in Poland, the Czech Republic, the former East Germany, and many other nations of the former Soviet bloc, the social and economic transformation brought about by freedom and decollectivization proved to be remarkable. Yet, today, an elite upper class reaps the majority of benefits generated by Russian capitalism. Increasingly, Russia is experiencing the problems associated with Western economies: concentration of capital and restrictions on freedom imposed by the capital cycle and its associated politics. As of late, Russia has also moved away from democratic reforms and embraced a greater degree of central control.

In Russia, we have a society that in living memory has experienced the strengths and weaknesses of socialism and capitalism, a nation that in every respect knows the machinery of scarcity-based economics. It is also a society that embodies a heritage of renewal. In Russia, we have an educated population that does not back down in the face of change and does not fear looking for a better way. Is Russia fertile ground for economics of fulfillment?

Our final situation as to the conditions needed to spark economic reformation is entirely different. It involves nations within a nation. When Europeans colonized North America, they encountered many indigenous peoples. To name the most recognized: in the East, colonists met the Shawnee, Iroquois, Delaware, and Illinois. In the Southeast: they met the Creek, Choctaw, Cherokee, and Seminole. On the plains: they met the Sioux, Mandan, Arapaho, Hidatsa, Comanche, Cheyenne, Shoshone, and Blackfoot. In the West and Northwest: they met the Ute, Modoc, Wasco, Yakama, Paiute, Spokane, Klamath, Chinook, Flathead, Okanagon, Salishan, Kottenai, Nez Percé, and Wallawalla.

At the time that it declared independence from England in 1776, one of the greatest problems the United States faced was how to deal with North America's indigenous peoples, many of whom had grown hostile toward white encroachment into tribal lands. In part, this situation resulted in Article I, Section 8, of the United States Constitution, which stated that: "The Congress shall have Power ... To regulate Commerce with foreign Nations, and among the several States, and with the Indian Tribes." This statement of law has and continues to shape the dealings of the United States Government with North America's native peoples.

In the late 1700s, settlers migrated across the Allegheny and Blue Ridge Mountains into what was then the Northwest Territory and is now Ohio, Kentucky, and Tennessee. The result was war with displaced Indians that in 1794 culminated with the Battle of Fallen Timbers in Ohio. Led by a Shoshone named Tecumseh, a coalition of Indian tribes met defeat against the revolutionary war hero General Anthony Wayne, known to his men as Mad Anthony. After the battle, Wayne negotiated the *Treaty of Greenville*, which set boundaries between land available for farming and "Indian Territory" and thus opened the Northwest Territory for settlement. The Treaty of Greenville also led to acts intended to reduce fraud and abuse in trade with Indian peoples and to acquire title to Native American land through negotiation as opposed to force.

The push to settle the West, however, overcame the government's attempts to manage the opening of the frontier. Many saw the Indian as an obstacle to progress, a nuisance to be exterminated. Others saw the Indian as a "redeemable savage" to be incorporated into society. Among the latter group was President Thomas Jefferson. Traditionally, the government had dealt with Indian peoples as sovereign nations. Jefferson ended this policy. He sought to bring the Indian into American society and encouraged church-run educational programs to teach native peoples to read and write and to turn them into farmers, ranchers, and carpenters.

The largely nomadic native population, however, resisted attempts at settlement; and, by the 1820s, the failure of Jefferson's approach had become clear. This led to the Indian Removal Act of 1830, which empowered President Andrew Jackson to move native peoples across the Mississippi. Though relocation was to be voluntary, the government had the power to compel Indians to move if necessary and orchestrated forced marches, often in the dead of winter.

By the middle of the nineteenth century, wagon trains had begun to roll west along the Oregon, Mormon, Santa Fe, and California trails. With the Great Plains open for homesteading, the government realized that to safeguard settlers it had to break up the vast reach of Indian Territory across the Mississippi. It adopted a pre-Jefferson policy of treating Indian peoples as sovereign nations, established reservations, and forced tribes to move onto these lands. This led to the Plains Indian Wars. Among these wars, were such battles as that led by then colonel George Armstrong Custer, who in 1876 at Little Bighorn met death and defeat at the hand of Sioux and Cheyenne warriors led by Sitting Bull and Crazy Horse. The

Plains Wars culminated in 1890 with the massacre of 300 Sioux men, women, and children at Wounded Knee in South Dakota, effectively ending Indian resistance to settlement.

In the course of the Plains Wars, Congress realized that the government needed a new Indian policy. It set aside the idea of treating Indian bands as sovereign nations dealt with through the treaty process and adopted native peoples as wards of the United States Government. This gave rise to the Dawes Act, or General Allotment Act, of 1887, which granted parcels of land to Indians with the intent that they settle down and learn to farm. Like Thomas Jefferson's "Redeemable Savage," the General Allotment act was an abject failure. By the start of the twentieth century, native peoples were among the nation's poorest.

In 1924, Congress granted Native Americans citizenship; and, in 1934, it passed the Indian Reorganization Act. This act, also called the "Indian New Deal," acknowledged the value of native culture. It encouraged groups to organize tribal governments and open tribal businesses. With some success in this area, congress resolved to treat Indians as any other American citizens and wean them from federal support. By the 1950s, the government had cut most federal funds for Native American affairs. Poverty on the reservations grew and forced many native people onto welfare. In the 1970s, Indian activists occupied Alcatraz Island in San Francisco Bay and the Bureau of Indian Affairs in Washington, D.C. These actions, and a seventy-one day armed siege at Wounded Knee, compelled the government to again rethink its Indian policy.

The pendulum of Native American policy continued its swing toward greater Indian independence, and the government adopted a strategy of self-determination that emphasized tribal administration of federally funded health, housing, education, welfare, and law enforcement programs. Today, the Federal government holds about 56 million acres in trust for 314 officially recognized tribes and groups. This includes 278 reservations in 35 states. At 16 million acres and with a population of 140 thousand people, the largest reservation is the Navajo, mostly in Arizona. At 0.25 acres and with, at the time of this writing, a population of six people, the smallest is the Golden Hill in Connecticut.

What is remarkable about the relationship between the United States Government and the country's Native peoples is the autonomy granted to Indians to manage their economic affairs. Under Article I, Section 8, of the United States Constitution, government has to some degree allowed native groups to operate outside the jurisdiction of the federal bureaucracy. In certain respects, reservations exist as they did a century ago, as sovereign nations within the territorial boundaries of the United States.

What is even more remarkable is the degree to which in recent years Indian peoples have made use of their sovereignty. Free from much of the taxation and much of the excessive social, land-use, and environmental restrictions that bog-down economic activity in the country as a whole, many Native American groups thrive as capitalists. They have built hotels, lodges, casinos, and other recreational facilities. They have opened stores that offer tax-free alcohol, tobacco, and other goods. Tribes fund business startups and higher education for members and have massed substantial pools of working capital.

Some Native Americans continue to see themselves as victims of past injustices and turn to the government and legal system for relief and subsistence. A growing number, however, have caught the entrepreneurial bug. Could these peoples living as citizens of nations within a nation— the descendents of those who while Europeans settled the New World subsisted as stone age hunters and gathers—lead the world in economic reformation?

We have described three situations that illustrate the conditions needed for economic reformation to take root. As different as these situations may be, they bring to light what is most important. Economic reformation is not a matter of politics, geography, and demographics, though these factors come into play. Economic reformation is a matter of imagination. To implement the first economics of fulfillment systems, we must adapt our model to the social and economic environment in which our economic system must function. By drawing on the power of our creativity, we can implement economics of fulfillment wherever we experience the need for freedom.

No matter how or where economics of fulfillment takes hold, the first economic systems will function as islands of liberty and abundance, as systems of hyper-creativity and free enterprise, importing and exporting to the outside economy. In time, however, the isolation of these economic units will end. Economics of fulfillment communities will grow and merge. As they do, they will reshape the economic landscape on a global scale.

At the heart of humanity's creation of a global economics of fulfillment structure is one, inescapable characteristic of an economics of fulfillment system with respect to its function in a socialist-capitalist economic environment. Under the economics of fulfillment framework, every individual has the freedom to participate in the economy to his or her potential. The individual devotes his or her energy to those activities that provide the greatest personal fulfillment. In terms of quality and innovation, therefore, a laborer in a socialist-capitalist business, who works for what may be little more than a subsistence level paycheck, could not out produce an individual in an economics of fulfillment business, a human being doing what he or she loves.

Our builder, for example, sold his house to the schoolteacher for 100 thousand dollars. This figure was based on the 50 thousand dollars he spent for materials and another 50 thousand dollars for land and labor. Because our builder can run a negative balance at our economics of fulfillment bank, however, he could as easily have sold his house for 75 or 50 thousand dollars, or given it away. Those in our economy have the freedom to produce the highest quality products and the freedom to charge as much or as little as they want without affecting their livelihood.

The outcome of this situation is inescapable. A business in a capitalist environment—bound by the ideology of scarcity and survival—cannot compete with a business in an economics of fulfillment environment. If price was not an issue, would you rather live in the architectural masterpiece created by our economics of fulfillment builder or in a banged-together tract house built by a profit-driven real estate developer? As the economics of fulfillment movement expands, businesses in the outside world, forced to live by a set of rules where there must be winners and losers, will face a growing threat from economics of fulfillment enterprises. This competitive situation will hasten the fall of traditional businesses. It will also encourage business owners to restructure jobs and improve working conditions so that they can conduct operations in an economics of fulfillment environment—which will encourage still more businesses to restructure operations and join the economics of fulfillment movement. Inherent in the economics of fulfillment philosophy is the means to catalyze its expansion.

The competitive situation in the private sector will also affect government. Like every member of our economics of fulfillment community, elected leaders and others in government can run a negative bank account balance or in some other way have access to capital. A tax structure to support government would be a needless accounting game. In the socialist-capitalist world, however, governments do not take taxes so lightly.

Nations fix taxes to economic activity: to usage, profit, income, sales price, and property value. As such, taxes paid by a member of an economics of fulfillment economy would be a source of capital outlay that, like any transfer of scarcity-based currency outside the economy, would be, in the self-directed management of the economy, minimized. Responsibly, a member of our economy will charge less for the outcome of his or her creative efforts, in particular on internal transactions where price has no real meaning. This downward price pressure along with the downward price pressure brought to bear by competition monetarily devalues the economic activity on which taxes are calculated. Traditional governments will find it harder and harder to collect revenue.

Pawns of those with power and wealth that they are, traditional governments will do what they can to end the economics of fulfillment threat to the tax base and to the profits of their overseers. To do this, governments will use the usual methods: regulation and police enforcement. When not faced with overt police and military actions, economics of fulfillment communities will confront legislation that attempts to force the valuation of goods and services based on the value of products in the scarcity-based environment. Many governments already impose a similar mandate on trade and bartering organizations. Economics of fulfillment communities will also face more desperate attempts to maintain the status quo of economic valuation. As profits and tax revenues decline, legislators will have little choice but to attempt to fix prices. This approach, however, challenges traditional economic function and, like attempts in the United States to fix prices during the inflationary times of the 1970s, will prove fundamentally unworkable. Conversely, as the private sector moves under the economics of fulfillment framework, government will attempt to stabilize prices by doing what it today does to run up prices—print money, which will further devalue the worth of scarcity-based economic activity and add to economic uncertainty.

Moreover, as tax revenues decline and governments fail to meet their social services obligations, citizens will grow increasingly disillusioned with government. Government may be the pawn of those with power and wealth, but it can only serve its masters with the consent of the people. From the standpoint of providing social services, government needs a dependent citizenry to justify its existence. As scarcity-based resources dwindle, more and more of those who rely on government for all or part of their livelihood will find it desirable to take jobs and start businesses in the economics of fulfillment framework. We will willingly walk away from government; and, when government loses our dependency, government loses its political base of authority.

Like the wrestler who uses the weight of his larger opponent against him, the economics of fulfillment movement turns the rules of scarcity-based economics against traditional economic structures and mechanisms of government. The Soviet Union and other socialist nations have fallen to humanity's drive to create less collective and more free and open societies. The socialist-capitalist economies that today define global economic activity, and the social structures they represent, will also fall to our drive to create more satisfying social arrangements. But unlike economic upheaval today, no one need be left behind. No one need leave his or her family to find work. No one need face hunger, unemployment, and homelessness. We all have the option of economic reformation.

Our growing freedom and the act of creating that freedom will carry us to a crossroads in our economic evolution. The time will come when our economics of fulfillment communities will reach the level of development where they no longer need to interact with traditional economies. We will have reached the point where our economics of fulfillment communities attain the size and diversity to form an independently functioning economic structure. No longer will economics of fulfillment systems exist in isolation. We will have wrapped the Earth in an economics of fulfillment matrix—a medium of freedom and creative expression, a landscape of heightened economic activity. This advance returns us to the topic of money, but not as we have thus far addressed it.

In time, socialism and capitalism will fall from dominance; and, with this development, the need for money in all its forms, past and present, will no longer exist. Never again will we monetarily value our creative efforts. Never again will we run a negative balance in our bank account. Our economics of fulfillment banks will have served their purpose, and we will shut them down. What remnants of the scarcity-based economy that remain will fall into history. The markets will close. The banking, investment, and insurance industries will cease operations. No more speculation. No more economic highs and lows. Government will abandon its role as an agent of central control, and new and traditional governments will merge under the economics of fulfillment framework. No more taxes.

No more budgets. No more surpluses and deficits. No more economic mandates and regulations. No more fiscal policy and monetary policy. No more classical economists and Keynesian economists. Humanity will have marked a turning point in its economic evolution. We will have transcended the usefulness of money.

And, with the creative energy expended to account for money unleashed, the creative process will propel social and cultural evolution in a new direction and to a new level of intensity. We will enter a period of unprecedented wealth and individual freedom—an age of never-before-experienced personal expression and material well-being. We will also enter an era of never-before-experienced social unity and purpose.

12

Social Reformation

FREE OF SCARCITY-BASED ECONOMICS and the demands of a monetary economy, the human community will enter a period of unprecedented freedom and material abundance. It will also enter a period of unprecedented personal and social well-being. What will life be like in the human societies of tomorrow? As far back in time as history and archeology allow us to probe, we as individuals and as a human community have unleashed suffering on one another. Are war and brutality intrinsic to human social change? Can we implement economics of fulfillment without the upheaval that throughout the ages has defined the emergence of a new social order?

As we have described, in the economics of fulfillment world of tomorrow there will be schools but not like the schools of today. There will be businesses but not like the businesses of today. There will be states, nations, and governments but not like the states, nations, and governments of today.

With respect to commerce, we will not base the size of a business on the need to accumulate capital or to limit competition and dominate market share but on the nature of the business. An airplane manufacturer will be large. It takes a lot of people and resources to build an airliner. Clothing manufacturers will be small. Rather than have chains of retail outlets controlling the distribution of clothing worldwide, each city will have hundreds if not thousands of independent garment makers producing original clothing of the finest quality and most innovative fabrics and designs. In our economics of fulfillment community, the form of a business will follow its function. Creativity rather than profit and market share will define business activity. To an extent scarcely imaginable under socialism-capitalism, our economy will be the domain of the entrepreneur and of the small business.

In this business climate, the nature of work will change. In a society where there is unlimited opportunity, a factory owner or other employer will not be able to find people willing to do repetitious work on an assembly line, or labor in any less than fulfilling situation. The solution is to reinvent work. Rather than have a half dozen automobile manufactures rolling out hundreds of thousands of units, we will have thousands of independent automobile builders handcrafting a few cars per year, building nothing but the best. In those instances where we cannot redesign work in this way, we will turn to technology. An engineer may realize his or her passion by building an automated assembly process. His or her creative outlet will be to advance the technology of production and to see to it that the production process runs smoothly. We will also reevaluate our expectations concerning work. If our passion is to own a restaurant and prepare and serve the finest meals, we must take the good with the bad. We will cook the best food and serve it in the most agreeable setting and on the most beautifully adorned tables, but we will also wash dishes. To realize our passion there are times when we must get our hands dirty.

As important, information will have a different meaning in the future. Today, surveillance cameras monitor our every move. Government and private agencies track our every e-mail, our every phone call, our every purchase. When business is no longer driven by competition and when government is no longer a mechanism of central control, there will be no reason to accumulate this type of data. As we have said, our builder must know the latest techniques of concrete construction, but he has no use for the credit rating of the person who buys his home. In our economy, marketing does not drive business. We do not need to identify customers and to target those whom we can coerce to buy. The vast databanks that store and distribute information on us will fall into obsolescence, and we will look back in disbelief at the complexity of our former lives. Data for the sake of data has no meaning. Knowledge is of value only when used to further our creative efforts—only when used to facilitate humankind's forward movement in evolution in whatever form that may manifest.

In this regard, the profession of journalism will have a new purpose. Reporters and commentators will no longer face corporate, government, and other political influences. When we abolish these restrictions and eliminate the profit motive, the role of the press changes. As it does today, the media will report events. But this will be the least important aspect of the journalistic endeavor. To a greater extent than at present—and in a much less superficial, ratings-oriented, politically driven way—the media will explore the meaning of events. To function in our economy, every member must have the information to responsibly conduct his or her affairs. The journalist of tomorrow will be driven by a calling to report and analyze the news in this context and as such will function as a component of our economy's information system. He or she will explore, question, and challenge. He or she will delve into events in light of our emerging evolution of consciousness view of our ourselves and of our universe. The journalist of tomorrow will bring to the profession an ethic of openness, understanding, and above all vision. He or she will take on journalism's most important role—the mission of evolutionary catalyst.

The absence of the laws and regulations needed to maintain economic function in the economics of fulfillment community has one other outcome—a situation most of us will be pleased to embrace. There is little need for a legal system and an enforcing body to make sure everyone plays by the rules. How much crime would we face and how big of a police force would we need if we eliminated illegal activities with an economic motivation? Today, courts and legislatures overwhelm the legal and criminal systems with tens of thousands of new laws, rulings, and regulations each year—many if not most politically motivated and many if not most redundant and unenforceable. In our economics of fulfillment system, the economic structure does not restrict economic behavior and limit freedom. It nurtures freedom and facilitates economic activity. Free from the need for central control, the rules of the economy are simple and reasonable. There is no incentive not to follow them, and little need for a legal system and an enforcing body to make sure we do.

In the future, we will live in cities, states, and nations. We will attend schools and pursue occupations. But rather than serve our professions and institutions, they will be the medium through which we fulfill our creative needs and, by our vision, the medium that allows us to facilitate the creative goals of others. We will engineer a world that catalyzes our capacity to learn and build. The life we are poised to create promises never-before-known freedom—avenues for personal betterment and creative expression limited only by our imagination.

In this world, we will interact as individuals and as a human community in more satisfying ways. To better understand this aspect of our future, we must examine a quality of the human experience that has per-vaded life since before recorded history, a dimension of who we are that, to achieve the awareness we need to overcome and evolve beyond, we must understand—*violent human conflict.* The turmoil of human interaction has many faces: crime, warfare, and terrorism. It has many catalysts: need, desperation, and fundamentalism. It also has an underlying nature, one that reveals itself by way of our evolution of consciousness view of the universe.

In the nonhuman world, conflict between members of a species establishes an individual's place within a social group and a group's place within the larger sphere of the ecosystem. Wolves fight among themselves for dominance in the pack. Packs defend their territory against neighboring packs. Traditionally, we have interpreted this conflict in the Darwinian framework of survival and competition. In light of our present understanding of the universe, this interpretation is not meaningful. Wolves and other animals do not fight to establish fitness and pass on their genes. Evolution is not driven by competition and the random process of natural selection.[1] This is only the view we have imposed on our observations of the natural world. For the wolf and other species, conflict takes place when members of a group shift position, or reestablish their place in wolf society. It also takes place when—faced with a drought, a shift in game migration, or some other form of environmental realignment—an ecosystem adjusts the interaction of groups within a species to maintain evolutionary equilibrium or to move between states of evolutionary equilibrium. Aggression is an aspect of evolution, a dimension of change—social and ecological.

The same idea applies to the human community. Before urbanization, violence within a group and violence between groups took place as in nonhuman societies. We fought for social position in our band and for our group's place with respect to other groups in an ecosystem, this defined by territory. Anthropological studies of hunting and gathering cultures suggest that this type of aggression was common but not to the extent that we might think. Social structure was simple and collective, and social status was not difficult to establish. Similarly, the ecological arrangement of groups was clearly defined. Aside from times of climate change or other ecological transition, each group had a place in the bio-

---

1. See *Book 1, Evolution of Consciousness*, chapters 10 and 13.

sphere and as such maintained established patterns of interaction. As long as a group respected the territory of neighboring groups there was little to fight about. In the nomadic, hunting and gathering culture, it was relatively easy to maintain social and ecological relationships.

Our drive to less collective social structure changed this state of existence. As groups became larger and social structures became more complex and interwoven, we found ourselves increasingly vying for power and social position within the group and increasingly driven to dominate neighboring groups in our quest to create less collective social arrangements. Egypt built an empire. Persia built an empire. Rome built an empire. Great Britain built an empire. In our look at Russian history, nomadic Slavic groups formed alliances to drive out Asian groups. As consciousness and social complexity increased, individuals interacted more politically and aggressively. To a greater extent than in the past, cultures extended their influence through military reach.

Moreover, with the advent of urbanization and the condition of scarcity that it brought into being, we fought to control resources. When Catherine the Great turned her armies against the Ottoman Empire to further her imperialistic dreams, she targeted Black Sea ports in warm waters where ships could enter year around. To advance his ideal of Arian dominance, Hitler fought for control of Polish, French, and Belgium coalfields and vied with the allies for control of Middle Eastern oil fields. Our drive to less collective social order entwined with our drive for resources and economic dominance. We battled for power, wealth, and material possession.

We also fought for ideology. What war is not waged in the name of a God? How many battles have we fought over an ideal of a deity, a passage of scripture, a notion of good and evil? How many campaigns have we engaged in over an economic philosophy—capitalism versus communism? Religious and other systems of belief placate our need for understanding. They allow us to internalize our behavior, to explain our world and by doing so to justify our ambition and aggression. Ideology allows us to enlist others in our cause and to fight for the greater good we feel our religious, economic, and other beliefs will bring to our families and to those whom we conquer.

On the evolution of consciousness level, the leading edge of evolution thrusts forward in time and the trailing edge of evolution reshapes earlier evolutionary forms in support of continued evolution, or if earlier forms are no longer needed allows them to fall from existence. We have a need to further evolution and a need to hold onto the past. But there are times when we stagnate.[2] There are times when, by virtue of our creative power, we cling to the past to such an extent that we hinder our evolution. Throughout history, a war has raged within us as individuals and as a human community. We are locked between poles—torn between the forces of past and future, novelty and fundamentalism, creativity and the way it has always been.

From the standpoint of the individual, there are times when we experience our battle to overcome stagnation as the thirst for power. There are also times when we satisfy our thirst for power through violence. History has given us countless leaders who—driven by the obsession to overcome the past—have forcibly propelled the world across the threshold to a new social order. Violence also arises when we have no outlet for our creativity. We turn to violence when we feel trapped and without hope. When, as evolving beings driven by the need to grow and learn, we face a social or economic situation that provides no avenue for us to express our need, we act according to our creative nature. We invent methods of release, and these methods may be violent.

From the standpoint of humanity, we can reduce the totality of human progress—good in the battle against evil, freedom in the battle against oppression, war and politics, victory and defeat, the call to rule and the call to follow, the drive to build and the drive to destroy—to humanity's struggle to defeat stagnation, to humanity's battle to build on and rise above the past to create the future. What historic event cannot be interpreted as a confrontation between those who want to create a better future, however they may define such, and those who want to maintain what has been, those who cling to power and to the ideals and social structures that sustain it?

In all its embodiments, violent human conflict is a manifestation of the creative mechanism. More overtly than any other form of human creative expression, violent human conflict is that which throughout history has marked humankind's movement through time. Violent human conflict is that which throughout the millennia has delineated humankind's rise out of the abyss of collectivity—that which has mapped humankind's

2. See *Book 1, Evolution of Consciousness*, chapters 10 and 11.

calling to, on the journey to meaning, lift itself to ever greater awareness and understanding. In the evolution of the universe to states of greater consciousness and fulfillment, violent human conflict is how the cycles and thresholds, the trial and error, the buildup and collapse of uncertainty, and the building on and creative discarding of the old that characterizes the fifteen-billion-year-old mechanism of the creative process has outwardly revealed itself.

And throughout the ages this manifestation of human creativity has taken place in abundance.

As early as 5,500 years ago, the Middle East from Egypt to Mesopotamia was in turmoil as rulers and empires rose and fell: Sumer, Egypt, Akkad, Babylon, Persia, Phoenicia, Palestine. In Greece, city-states fought for dominance as they made and broke alliances in constant battles against one another, culminating with the rise of Macedonia and the conquest of the known world by Alexander the Great. In Rome, nobles quarreled among themselves while legions built an empire with the javelin, the short sword, and the technique of the siege.

The decline of the Roman Empire swept humanity into the Middle Ages. The Avars and Bulgars marched on the remnants of Ancient Rome from the east, and the Vikings advanced from the north. Magyar forces advanced from the lower Danube, and the Moors and other Islamic forces advanced from the Middle East. Western Europeans dealt with these raids by creating a feudal system where the aristocracy took on the responsibility for defense. In the fourteenth and fifteenth centuries, feudalism gave way to the nation-state—with its kings, armies, and bureaucracies. China, Africa, Australia, the South Pacific, and the New World have their own stories of conflict, with the aggression of European nations woven into the plot. In the late nineteenth and early twentieth century, a global economy emerged. The reach of nations expanded, and World Wars I and II founded an order of nations.

Distance in time may allow us to judge our past as brutal, but it is our heritage. It has sculpted the landscape of humanity's ascent out of collectivity. Without social transformation—as cruel and remorseless as its manifestation has been—today's emerging global community would not exist. We would not have the foundation on which to build the more nestled, satisfying, and strongly bonded social arrangements of the future.

This said, is violent conflict an unavoidable outcome of human social evolution? From our discussion thus far, we might conclude that violence is intrinsic to social change—that societies cannot evolve without the turmoil that throughout history has accompanied social reorganization. Can we re-shape human society into more satisfying forms without violence? Can we bring economics of fulfillment to the world without pain and turmoil?

Throughout history, humanity has advanced blindly forward in time. Tension has built within a society to the point where uncertainty has overwhelmed and a new social order has emerged from the rubble of social and economic breakdown. As, by way of humanity's ascendance, the universe crosses the threshold to meaning, this sequence of events is not immutable. This expression of the creative dynamic is not absolute.

Change unfolds through the cycles and thresholds, the trial and er-ror, and the creative building on and discarding of the old of the creative process. Our understanding of the creative process, our knowledge of the mechanism of change, gives us the means to control the creative process. Our internalization of the universe, our consciousness of how and for what purpose we came to be, empowers us to manage the evolutionary dynamic. Our ascendance to wisdom gives us the vision to command the battle between evolution's leading and trailing arrows, the insight to see stagnation for what it is and by doing so to rise above it. Our tran-scendence enables us to manipulate the creative dynamic, to manage the buildup and release of uncertainty, to take command of the trial and error and building on and discarding of the old of creativity—to in a coherent way bring forth our future.

We need not advance blindly forward in time. We need not face the buildup and collapse of uncertainty. We need not take as immutable the fifteen billion year old mechanism of the creative process. We can reshape human society into more satisfying forms without violence. We can end war and brutal human interaction. We can reinvent global economics without pain. We can bring economics of fulfillment to the world without suffering.

But will we?

In the economics of fulfillment world of tomorrow, economic fac-tions will not be in opposition, and government will not dominate our lives. Without money, we will have no economic crime and little need for a criminal justice system. In the world we are poised to create, we will not compete for resources, and those driven by dreams of power and mate-rial acquisition will not have the means to enlist the allegiance of others. How many revolutions has poverty spawned? How many armies has the dream of conquest raised? How many acts of terror has hopelessness inspired? How many religious orders has our need for salvation brought into being?

Our future is clear. Our road to that future is not. As in the past, we can rush blindly forward in time and pay the price in social disintegration and human suffering. But events need not unfold in this way. We know where we are, and we know where we want to be. To avoid the war and torment that throughout history has characterized human progress, we need only devise the best way to get there. We need only take it on ourselves to control the creative process, to command the creative dynamic, to manage the buildup and release of uncertainty, to engineer the best possible path to the world of tomorrow. Our future stands before us, awaiting our inventiveness. A global economics of fulfillment community and the human evolution that it embodies will rise out of conscious action or out of the ashes of social and economic meltdown. The choice and the responsibility are ours.

13

Obsolescence of Economics

IN WHATEVER WAY MEANING unfolds in the human community, our economics of fulfillment ideology will play a role. Our economic philosophy is an outcome of evolution and establishes the environment in which human creativity can most dramatically take place. Economics of fulfillment provides the freedom to live as we deem meaningful and to redefine our ambitions as we grow and learn. As this advancement comes about, heightened freedom on Earth will bring us to yet another turning point in our economic evolution. Like socialism and capitalism, economics of fulfillment is a transitional ideology, a step along the way. Economics of fulfillment will allow us as individuals and as a human community to progress to an even more evolved form of economic interaction.

In the nomadic hunting and gathering culture, economics did not dominate our thoughts and activities. Economics was not the focal point of life, the end-and-all of existence. This changed as evolution spawned less collective forms of social structure, and our ancestors found it desirable to build permanent settlements. In the early urban community, we existed removed from the plains and forests that provided for our material needs. As a result, the settlement experienced a state of intrinsic scarcity of resources, and we were compelled to devise ways to gather goods in the countryside, where they existed in surplus, and to transport them into the settlement, where they existed in deficit. Urbanization founded scarcity-based economics—economic doctrine rooted in the belief that resources are by nature limited and human material wants are by nature unlimited.

At its essence, a scarcity-based economic system is a way to regulate human behavior. It is an agreed upon method of conducting subsistence activities based on a mutually accepted view of the world. To some extent, regulation took care of itself through supply and demand, through what we today would call market forces. Left to the dictates of the market, however, some members of the community would have more than they needed and others would not have enough. This disparity of wealth would create tension, and the social structure of the community would lose cohesiveness. To maintain the integrity of the community, and thus to further humankind's evolution to greater individuality and less collective social forms, everyone's needs had to be met, at least to the standards agreed on by the community. There had to be rules to direct individual behavior for the common good. For the community to be a community, some form of central control was also necessary.

Central control, of course, required that someone be in charge, that someone make the rules everyone else had to follow. As communities grew larger and the need for resources grew more pressing, a ruling, or governing, class took on the responsibility to figure out what was needed, who did what, and who received the benefits. Those who made the rules had to have a way to make everyone else abide by the rules. This led to the emergence of an enforcing class and to what today we would call the police state. The ruling class governed. The enforcing class enforced. But, in the pure sense, neither group directly contributed to the material well-being of the community. Most in the community found themselves members of the working class.

Scarcity had other, equally profound outcomes. It framed our observations of the natural world and by doing so structured the way we interacted with our environment. We came to see the universe in terms of our struggle to survive, in terms of our conflict with what we deemed Earth and nature. As important, scarcity brought into being the concept of work and labor. With scarcity, subsistence increasingly became work and we increasingly became laborers. Scarcity also brought into being concepts of wealth and property and nurtured the idea of competition, the notion that for every winner there must be one or more losers.

As the ages unfolded, the view of the world spawned by humanity's move from a nomadic to an urban way of life and the condition of scarcity that it created gave rise to a number of economic practices and to a number of economic philosophies and philosophers. With regard to the evolution of our economic practices and ideologies, we discern a trend, one that we traced and expanded on throughout the book. From mercantilism and Adam Smith to laissez-faire and classical economics, from Marx and Darwin to neoclassical and Keynesian economics, as human social structure rose out of collectivity, economic systems and theories evolved from those that embraced more central control and less individual freedom to those that embraced less central control and more individual freedom.

In the course of our economic progress, Darwin's natural selection model of evolution furthered a materialistic view of the world and our devotion to the economic ideologies at work today: free market economics in the form of capitalism and planned economics in the form of socialism. Our scarcity-based, socialist-capital universe, however, poises on the brink of change. Our knowledge of the world, and the technology our knowledge has allowed us to create, has rendered the concept of resource scarcity obsolete. With this realization, we take the first step beyond a scarcity-based interpretation of the universe and the economic beliefs and practices that this view has inspired. We face the obsolescence of socialism and capitalism and the opportunity to devote our creative energy to a new economic philosophy, to an ideology rooted in the evolution of consciousness vision of the universe and in the acceptance of the creative nature and inherent worth of the human being. We embrace an economics of fulfillment.

> The objective of the Economics of Fulfillment ideology is to create the social and economic conditions that provide the freedom and opportunity for every individual to evolve to his or her highest state of being and that by doing so allow humanity to evolve to its highest state of being.

Economics of fulfillment is the ideology that those who are troubled by injustice and economic inequality and who envision a more peaceful and cooperative world seek but cannot find in socialism. Economics of fulfillment is the ideology that those who are troubled by government control and regulatory intrusion into our lives and who envision a world of greater freedom and entrepreneurialism seek but cannot find in capitalism. It is the economic system of beliefs that, when we look with open eyes, we long to create and dearly wish to live under, the economic philosophy that the unfolding of existence has led us to desire—the next step in our economic evolution.

As for the guiding principle of our economics of fulfillment ideology, we can devise many systems of economic practice that function beneath its blanket. In the previous chapters, we proposed what may be the simplest. We developed an economic model that provided every member of the economy with the opportunity to achieve his or her creative objectives through the mechanism of running a negative balance in his or her bank account. As basic and as impractical as this may seem, and in one sense it is nothing more than an accounting gimmick, it allowed us to explore the feasibility of our system, to contrast past economic practices with future economic practices, and to lay out the steps necessary to implement our economic ideology.

It also allowed us to outline the educational system needed to sustain an economics of fulfillment community. Traditional education is designed to invoke social and political conformity and to output the labor part of land, labor, and capital. Our economics of fulfillment model requires an open and diverse educational system, one that prepares every member of the economy to manage his or her economic activities in an enlightened way. As such, our educational system must provide us with the opportunity to discover our passion in life, and it must make available the skills and educational resources we need to realize that passion.

Our simple economic model also allowed us to contrast contemporary government with government as we will practice it in the future. Today, the dominant function of government is economic control. Tomorrow, the responsibility for economic regulation will rest with the individual. Factions will no longer be at odds with one another and with society, and we will no longer face the preponderance of laws and regulations needed to keep interests in line and the economy from unraveling. Today, we maintain a primitive, often corrupt form of democracy—the facade of democracy. Tomorrow, we will practice democracy where the freedom of the many is realized through the freedom of the individual—democracy given form by our creative expression and vision of the future. Throughout history, the power of government has shifted from the few to the masses. This trend is poised to continue in the most significant way. The power of government will shift from the masses to every individual.

Conceivably, the first economics of fulfillment systems could emerge anywhere in the world. Citizens of all nations will play a role, and the possibilities as to which peoples will take the lead are limited only by our imagination. No matter where the first economics of fulfillment communities begin, as they expand and merge they will turn the forces of scarcity-based economics against traditional economic practices, and we will find it increasingly difficult to function in the pure capitalistic sense—to make money off of money and the labor of others. As economics of fulfillment spreads, the remnants of socialism and capitalism will fall into history. The markets will close. The banking, investment, and insurance industries will shutdown. New and traditional governments will merge, and government will abandon the role of a regulatory body. Never again will we use currency to conduct a transaction. Evolution will have liberated humankind from the burden of money.

With the energy expended to account for money unleashed, we will enter a period of never before known wealth and material abundance. We will also enter a period of never before known social unity and purpose. With this insight comes the choice we face today. Our future is clear, but our path to that future is not. Throughout history, social transformation has unfolded as it may. Like a driver who never looks beyond the hood of the car, we have advanced blindly through the ages. We can opt to let the creative process unfold as it has done in the past. A less collective global society and the economics of fulfillment economy it will support will emerge after the collapse of our old way of life and the turmoil and human suffering such a collapse will bring. But evolution need not progress in this way. Our understanding of the universe and its evolution empowers us to take control of the creative process. We grasp humanity's role in evolution. We know where we are headed and need only draft and execute the best possible plan to get there. The choice is ours. We can let uncertainty build within the human community until it overwhelms, or we can recognize the buildup of uncertainty for what it is and manage its release—channel its energy in the way we determine best. We can engineer the road to our future.

Whether we choose to take command of the creative dynamic or to let events and the cycles and thresholds, trial and error, and buildup and collapse of uncertainty that defines the creative process unfold as they have always done, the outcome will be the same. In the evolution of our economic beliefs and practices, we will embrace the economics of fulfillment ideology and implement systems that adhere to the principles embodied in that ideology. As we do, we will cross the threshold to meaning and in time to a still more inspiring economic form.

Twelve thousand years ago, humankind broke away from a nomadic hunting and gathering subsistence pattern and began an urban way of life. In one sense, economics of fulfillment will bring us full-circle. In the hunting and gathering culture, economics did not dominate life. Economic activity took place, but economics was not what life was about. Like socialism and capitalism, economics of fulfillment is a transitional ideology, but there will be no economic philosophy or economic models to replace it. As economic reformation spreads to embrace the planet, we will evolve beyond our need for the ideology that made economic rebirth possible. Humanity will have liberated itself from material burden to such an extent that economics itself will be an obsolete notion—a topic studied by the historian but, like any event distant in time, worthy of exploration but never truly understood. We will have evolved beyond economics to create a world of unprecedented unity and opportunity, a place of never-before-known freedom, individuality, and material expression. In all its forms, economics will have fallen into the past—taken refuge in the sanctity of history, descended into the realm of evolution's trailing arrow.

14

Mission for Change

IT IS MY BELIEF that today the universe is crossing what I call the threshold to meaning. This threshold unfolds within the human being and represents the most profound evolutionary advance since the emergence of reflective consciousness more than one hundred thousand years ago. The transcendence now underway will reshape our lives on many levels. Among these levels will be the reinvention of economic philosophy and the emergence of new forms of economic practice based on that philosophy. As an individual, what role do we play in economic rebirth? What is our place in economic reformation, our mission for change?

The future to which we aspire is clear. Ahead, we find economics of fulfillment—an economic ideology based on the principle that humanity, and thus the universe, can achieve its potential only when every human being has the freedom and opportunity to achieve his or her potential. Yet the economics of tomorrow is more than a framework of beliefs, more than a philosophy of allocation and production. Economics of fulfillment is an outcome of evolution. It is a manifestation of our rise to greater consciousness and less collective forms of social structure, a catalyst in the universe's becoming. Economics of fulfillment is the economic system of beliefs that, when we pause to reflect, we want to live and work within. It is the economic philosophy that embodies the ideals that those who embrace the value of the human being on the political left and political right have long sought but cannot find in Marxism or capitalism. Our economic ideology provides the framework to fulfill our material needs and our more deeply felt needs of creativity and individuality—our needs as evolving beings in an evolving universe.

To create the economy of tomorrow and the more satisfying personal and social way of life that it embodies, however, we must put the present behind us. In today's world, we find scarcity-based economics in the form of socialism and capitalism, and the melding of these practices that characterizes the economies of all nations and jurisdictions. Socialism and capitalism are systems of economic belief based on a materialistic view of the universe brought into being by the human move to urbanization and furthered by the mechanistic ideals of traditional science and Darwinian natural selection. In today's world, we value the accumulation of wealth over creative expression and the generation of wealth. As a result, we live in a global community dominated by economic power and by the social status and class structure economic power defines. The world of today offers a way of life gripped by an obsolete understanding of the universe and the economic ideologies it supports, but one we have grown to accept.

Caught up in the uncertainty of our time, we struggle to find our way. We know where we are at and where we want to be, but we do not know how to get there. Our future is clear, but the road to that future awaits our invention. The process of innovation takes place when we as individuals provide ourselves with the freedom to grow and learn, with the room to evolve to new levels of insight and wisdom. As such, the reformation of global economics begins in the humblest of ways. To reinvent global economics we must permit our thoughts to take us where they may. To initiate economic rebirth, we must open ourselves to the possibility that we can imagine and implement a better system of economic beliefs and practices, a system that will allow us to create a more satisfying way of life. Economic reformation begins within—by our search for what we take to be meaningful.

From this most unpretentious of beginnings comes the drive to question and the urge to reflect on all that we read and hear. Like the teacher in our economics of fulfillment educational system, we must look beneath the surface. We must figure out how things work and define the assumptions and motivations on which they are based. We must question existing economic practices. We must challenge the concepts put forth in these pages. Only when we delve into these ideas with a critical mind can we refine them in such a way that we make them our own.

When we free our power of reflection, our life aligns with the flow of the universe's evolution. We become a member of the human community who is conscious of the evolution of the human community and thus who knows its ultimate outcome and the path we as human beings must pursue to achieve that outcome. We have made the decision to bring forth our future without the conflict that in the past has defined social reorganization. Insight by insight, we draft the design for economic reformation. Empowered by our individuality and by the unity with others it allows us to achieve, we take command of the evolutionary dynamic and engineer the road to our future.

Bibliography

Anderson, Richard D., et al. *Post Communism and the Theory of Democracy*. Princeton, NJ: Princeton University Press, 2001.

Andrews, Charles. *From Capitalism to Equality: An Inquiry into the Laws of Economic Change*. Oakland, CA: Needle Press, 2000.

Aslund, Anders. *Russia's Capitalist Revolution: Why Market Reform Succeeded and Democracy Failed*. Washington, DC: Peter G. Peterson Institute for Economics, 2007.

Bergson, Henri. *Creative Evolution*. Translated by Arthur Mitchell. New York: The Modern Library, 1944.

Bergson, Henri. *The Creative Mind*. Translated by Mabelle L. Andison. New York: Greenwood Press, 1968.

Bergson, Henri. *Time and Free Will: An Essay on the Immediate Data of Consciousness*. Translated by F. L. Pogson. New York: Greenwood Press, 1968.

Brockway, George. *The End of Economic Man: An Introduction to Humanistic Economics*. New York: Norton, 2001.

Campbell, Bernard G. *Humankind Emerging, 7th ed*. New York: HarperCollins, 1996.

Caplan, Brian. *The Myth of the Rational Voter: Why Democracies Choose Bad Polices*. Princeton, NJ: Princeton University Press, 2007.

D'Amato, Paul. *The Meaning of Marxism*. Chicago: Haymarket Books, 2003.

Darwin, Charles. *On the Origin of Species*. New York: New American Library, 1958.

Delfgaauw, Bernard. *Evolution: The Theory of Teilhard de Chardin*. Translated by Hubert Hoskins. New York: Harper and Row, 1969.

Dimensions of Mind. Edited by Sidney Hook. New York: Collier Books, 1961.

Dodson, Edward O. *The Teilhardian Synthesis, Lamarckism & Orthogenesis*. Lewisburg, VA: American Teilhard Association, 1993.

Dubos, René. *Celebrations of Life*. New York: McGraw-Hill, 1981.

Ekelund, Robert and Robert Tollison. *Mercantilism as a rent-seeking Society: Economic Regulation in Historical Perspective*. College Station, TX: Texas A&M Press, 1981.

Fabra, Paul. *Capitalism Versus Anti-Capitalism: The Triumph of Ricardism*. Piscataway, NJ: Transaction Publishers, 1993.

Farb, Peter. Humankind: *What We Know About Ourselves. Where We Came From And Where We Are Headed. Why We Behave The Way we do*. New York: Bantam, 1978.

Giere, Ronald N. *Understanding Scientific Reasoning, 3rd ed*. Austin, TX: Holt, Rinehard, and Winston, 1991.

Grenet, Paul. *Teilhard de Chardin: The Man and His Theories*. Translated by R. A. Rudorff. London: Souvenir Press, 1965.

Hurley, Patrick J. *A Concise Introduction to Logic, 5th ed*. Belmont, VA: Wadsworth Publishing Company, 1994.

Bibliography

Huxley, Julian. *New Bottles for New Wine*. New York: Harper and Brothers, 1957.

Jantsch, Erich. *Design for Evolution: Self-Organization and Planning in the Life of Human Systems*. New York: Braziller, 1975.

Jantsch, Erich. *The Evolutionary Vision: Toward a Unifying Paradigm of Physical, Biological, and Sociocultural Evolution*. Boulder, CO: Westview Press for the American Association for the Advancement of Science, 1981.

Jantsch, Erich. *The Self-Organizing Universe: Scientific and Human Implications of the Emerging Paradigm of Evolution*. New York: Pergamon Press, 1980.

Jones, Steven, R. D. Martin, and David Pilbeam. *The Cambridge Encyclopedia of Human Evolution*. Cambridge, UK: Cambridge University Press, 1992.

Keynes, John Maynard. *A Treatise on Money*. New York: AMS Press, 1976.

Keynes, John Maynard. *The Economic Consequences of Peace*. New York: Harcourt Brace, 1920.

Keynes, John Maynard. *The General Theory of Employment, Interest and Money*. New York: Harcourt Brace, 1935.

King, Ursula. *Christ in All Things: Exploring Spirituality with Teilhard de Chardin*. Maryknoll, NY: Orbis Books, 1997.

Lane, David. *The Phenomenon of Teilhard: Prophet for a New Age*. Macon, GA: Mercer University Press, 1996.

Maass, Allen. *The Case for Socialism*. Chicago: Haymarket Books, 2005.

Malthus, Thomas Robert. *An Essay on the Principle of Population*. Homewood, IL: Richard D. Irwin, 1963.

Malthus, Thomas Robert. *Definitions in Political Economy*. New York: A. M. Kelly, 1963.

Marx, Karl. *Capital, A Critique of Political Economy*. New York: The Modern Library, 1906.

Marx, Karl. *A Contribution to the Critique of Political Economy*. New York: International Publishers, 1970.

Marx, Karl. *The Communist Manifesto*. Chicago: H. Regency Co., 1954.

McComish, Bruce. *Antilogic: Why Businesses Fail and Individuals Succeed*. New York: Wiley, 2001.

Mill, John Stuart. *Principles of Political Economy*. New York: McGraw Hill, 1973.

Munck, Ronald and Denis O'Hearn. *Critical Development Theory: Contributions to a New Paradigm*. New York: St. Martin's Press, 1999.

Myrdal, Gunnar. *Against the Stream: Critical essays on Economics*. New York: Pantheon. 1973.

Newman, Michael. *Socialism: A Very Short Introduction*. New York: Oxford University Press, 2005.

Norris, Robert E. and L. Lloyd Haring. *Political Geography*. New York: Charles E. Merril and Company, 1980.

Orega y Gasset, José. *The Revolt of the Masses*. New York: W. W. Norton and Company, 1960.

Peterson, Willis. *Principles of Economics, 4th ed*. Homewood, IL: Richard D. Irwin, 1980.

Pletsch, Carl. *Young Nietzsche: Becoming a Genius*. New York: The Free Press, 1991.

Prigogine, Ilya and Isabelle Stengers. *Order Out of Chaos*. New York: Bantam, 1984.

Putterman, Louis. *Dollars and Change: Economics in Context*. New Haven, CT: Yale University Press, 2001.

Ricardo, David. *Principles of Political Economy and Taxation*. New York: Dutton, 1973.

Bibliography

Schneider, Herbert Wallace. *Adam Smith's Moral and Political Philosophy*. New York: Harper and Row, 1948.

Schumpeter, Joseph. *Business Cycles: A theoretical, Historical, and Statistical Analysis of the Capitalistic Process*. New York: McGraw Hill, 1964.

Smith, Adam. *An Inquiry Into The Nature and Causes of the Wealth of Nations*. New York: P. F. Collier and Son, 1910.

Smith, Adam. *The Theory of Moral Sentiments*. Indianapolis, IN: Liberty Classics, 1976.

Sowell, Thomas. *Basic Economics 3rd Edition: A Common Sense Guide to the Economy*. New York: Basic Books, 2007.

Stamps, Normal L. *Why Democracies Fail: A Critical Evaluation of the Causes of Modern Dictatorships*. Notre Dame, IN: University of Notre Dame Press, 1957.

Swanson, Christopher B, *Cities in Crisis: A Special Analytic Report on High School Graduation*. Bethesda, MD: Editorial Projects in Education, 2008.

Teilhard de Chardin, Pierre. *Activation of Energy*. Translated by Rene Hague. London: Collins, 1970.

Teilhard de Chardin, Pierre. *Building the Earth*. Translated by Noel Lindsay. Wilkes-Barre, PA: Dimension Books, 1965.

Teilhard de Chardin, Pierre. *Christianity and Evolution*. Translated by Rene Hague. New York: Harcourt Brace Jovanovich, 1971.

Teilhard de Chardin, Pierre. *Early Man of China*. New York: AMS Press, 1980.

Teilhard de Chardin, Pierre. *Human Energy*. Translated by J. M. Cohen. London: Collins, 1969.

Teilhard de Chardin, Pierre. *Hymn of the Universe*. Translated by Gerald Vann. New York: Harper and Row, 1961.

Teilhard de Chardin, Pierre. *Let Me Explain*. Edited by Jean-Pierre Demoulin. Translated by Rene Hague. London: Collins, 1970.

Teilhard de Chardin, Pierre. *Letters From a Traveller*. New York: Harper and Row, 1962.

Teilhard de Chardin, Pierre. *Letters to Two Friends*. 1926-1952: New York: New American Library, 1968.

Teilhard de Chardin, Pierre. *Man's Place in Nature*. Translated by Rene Hague. New York: Harper and Row, 1966.

Teilhard de Chardin, Pierre. *On Love and Happiness*. San Francisco: Harper and Row, 1984.

Teilhard de Chardin, Pierre. *Science and Christ*. Translated By Rene Hague. New York: Harper and Row, 1968.

Teilhard de Chardin, Pierre. *The Appearance of Man*. Translated by Robert T. Francoeur. New York: Harper and Row, 1965.

Teilhard de Chardin, Pierre. *The Divine Milieu: An Essay on the Interior of Life*. New York: Harper and Row, 1960.

Teilhard de Chardin, Pierre. *The Future of Man*. Translated by Norman Denny. New York: Harper and Row, 1964.

Teilhard de Chardin, Pierre. *The Heart of the Matter*. Translated by Rene Hague. New York: Harcourt Brace Jovanovich, 1979.

Teilhard de Chardin, Pierre. *The Letters of Teilhard de Chardin and Lucile Swan*. Edited by Mary W. Gilbert. Washington, DC: Georgetown University Press, 1993.

Teilhard de Chardin, Pierre. *The Making of a Mind: Letters from a Soldier-Priest, 1914-1919*. Translated by Rene Hague. New York: Harper and Row, 1965.

Bibliography

Teilhard de Chardin, Pierre. *The Phenomenon of Man*. Translated by Bernard Wall. New York: Harper and Row, 1959.

Teilhard de Chardin, Pierre. *The Vision of the Past*. Translated by J. M. Cohen. London: Collins, 1966.

Teilhard de Chardin, Pierre. *Toward the Future*. Translated By Rene Hague. New York: Harcourt Brace Jovanovich, 1975.

Teilhard de Chardin, Pierre. *Writings in Time of War*. Translated By Rene Hague. New York: Harper and Row, 1968.

Wallerstine, Immanuel Maurice. *The Modern World-System II: Mercantilism and the Consolidation of the European World-Economy*. New York: Academic Press, 1980.